WEAPONS OF
MASS PRODUCTION

21 Days to Uncommon Productivity with God

WEAPONS OF MASS PRODUCTION

21 Days to Uncommon Productivity with God

Carlton Reed

Bible quotations are from the New International Version (NIV), King James Version
(KJV), The Amplified Bible (AMP), or the author's translation.

ISBN 978-061-587026-7

Weapons of Mass Production: 21 Days to Uncommon Productivity with God

Printed in the United States of America, 2011.
First Edition

Publisher – Inspirational International, Inc.
Cover Design – Interprint Communications, Inc.
Photography – Jerome King /Clear Image Photography
Editor – Alvelyn Sanders
Copy Editor – Houston Hawley

Table of Contents

Acknowledgments

This project would not be possible were it not for the assistance of some very special people. There are so many who have been helpful with this book, it would be impossible to thank them all.

I would like to thank, first and foremost, my Savior Jesus Christ for his leadership, example, and direction. This book is dedicated to Him for giving us a model to live by.

To my pastors, Dr. Creflo A. Dollar, Jr. and Pastor Taffi L. Dollar, of World Changers Church International, thank you for living the life before me and for letting your lives be the greatest sermon ever preached. You have truly made an indelible mark on my life, which can never be erased.

To my father, June Reed, I thank you for never giving up on me, and instilling in me a true work ethic. Watching you lead in the workforce was one of the chief motivations for this book. Thank you for your love.

To my mother, and world's greatest inspirer and cheerleader, Sylvia Reed, I say thank you Mom. You are the world's most amazing mother! I have never been in your presence, and not felt like I could fly! Thanks for paying the price.

To my older brother, Charles, thanks for the fine example you set for me as a young man, who in college, decided to live seriously for God!

To my brother, Tracy, you are a rock! What a tremendous example you are of a warrior for God! Thanks for your friendship and counsel. If I ever see you and a bear in a fight, I will be sure to help that poor bear!

To my brother, Mayor Kasim Reed, you are an inspiration to us all! Thank you for your love and kindness, and for showing the world what leadership looks like. You are just getting warmed up!

To my son Christian, thanks for the privilege of being your Dad. You are a great young Man of God, and a great example for young people all over to follow. You are destined for greatness, and I am so proud of you!

To my dream scout sister, and publicist, Marjé Etheridge, thanks for believing in me from the beginning, and pushing me into my destiny with your encouraging words.

Thank you to my friend and mentor, Jimmie Lucas, Jr. for your tireless commitment to encourage men to be true Men of God.

To my wonderful sister in Christ, Rebecca Watkins, I thank you for having faith in me, and in this book.

To Verda Watson, thank you for your support during this project.

To Deb Sorgel, thank you for your love and kindness.

To Jenessa Waddlington, thank you for your help and generosity.

Thank you to my friend, Rev. Dr. Pauline Fuller for your great friendship and ministry of word and song.

Thank you to my friend Joel Casoria and the entire staff at Trinity Broadcasting for your love and support.

To my stepmother, Dr. Rogsbert Phillips Reed, thanks for your love and support.

To my sister-in-law, Crystal Reed, thanks for always being my biggest fan.

To my editor, Alvelyn Sanders, thank you for helping to shape this book and give it a personality all its own. You breathed life into this project!

To my copy editor, Houston Hawley, you are one of the most brilliant editors, and one of the smartest people I know! God bless you. You have genius beyond your years!

To my friend Casey Hawley, thank you for your honesty, genius, and encouragement as I wrote this book. For this book to win the respect of your renowned literary mind and gifts is beyond me.

Many thanks to Monica Maldonado and Interprint Communications, Inc. for providing exactly the right cover design. Thanks to you and Raphael for your friendship and tireless support.

Thanks to Jan Bryson and Dwayne Heard for your cheers.

To Dr. Georgianne Thomas, thanks for encouraging me to dream and reach higher.

To Ambassador Andrew Young, thank you for your life of service.

To Pastor James Powers, my longtime pastor, friend, and mentor, thank you for being a father and for teaching me to walk with God

To my uncle and aunt, Doctors Harrison B. Wilson and Lucy Wilson, thank you for your never-ending confidence in me, and for hosting me at Norfolk State University.

To Sarah Grace Kiffin, affectionately known as "Mama Grace," thanks for all of the love!

To Curtis and Carmalinda Collins and family, you are the greatest. Thanks for the great support and fellowship. Thank you for allowing me to camp out at your house, whether writing, laughing, fellowshipping or praying.

Thank you to my great friend and brother, Darcy Ogandaga and your lovely wife, Danita.

Thanks for your confidence in me, and for helping me to take this message worldwide.

To my aunt and Godmother, Roena Littlejohn, thank you for loving and believing in me as long as I can remember.

To my aunt, Dorothy Anderson, you are unconditional love personified.

Thanks to my great friend, and intercessor, La'lla Walker for encouraging me to seek a higher walk with God.

Thank you to Pam Carter for your tireless support and excellence. You are a first class lady.

To my longtime friend, fellow speaker and author, Jonathan Williams, thanks for hanging in there with me buddy, you are the best.

Thank you to Dennis Zakas and Lou Zakas for their assistance with this book.

Many Thanks to Dr. Dennis Kimbro for your encouragement.

And to everyone who marches boldly into the workforce worldwide to make an impact for God, thank you!

Preface

A Soldier's Story

We have many callings in life. What has God called you to do? Have you found that thing for which you were created? Without question, you have a calling in life, a special plan that God has given you to fulfill, something that you were born to do. Even Jesus knew that He had a calling in life. In fact, upon being asked if He were a king, Jesus responded with these words: "Toward this end was I born." It is vitally important that we understand that we have not only **a calling,** but **callings** in life.

Our multiple callings are a spiritual example of "multi-tasking" at its best. There is the calling of being a father, who leads and guides his household for God. There is the calling of being a mother, who raises, nurtures, and teaches children to be productive members of society. There is the calling of civic responsibility in the community, and the calling to one's profession or job. You are called to wear many hats, and to do many things in life. However, above all things, you must always understand that you are called to be a soldier in the army of God.

No matter what we do or encounter in life, we must always maintain the mentality of a soldier, and always be ready for combat. This is not optional! The problem in our society today is that we have forgotten that we are at war! Still not convinced? Listen to these military terms, and see if they sound familiar to you.

"Fight the good fight of faith!"

"Put on the whole armor of God."

"Occupy until I come!"

"Pursue, overtake, and without fail, recover all."

"Having done all to stand, stand!"

Listen to those great combat phrases. Why do you think God uses them in the Bible? It is because, like Jesus, you and I were born for war. We are called to be more than conquerors through Christ who loved us.

This truth alone does not guarantee our success. There is something more that God requires of you in order for you to truly be a winner, and it is this: A decision! You must decide whether you will be the conqueror, or the conquered. A choice must be made in order for you to win! You must decide to serve God by accepting the high calling of being a soldier for Christ. What does it mean to be a soldier for Christ? It means that we can never put this profession down. It means that it is not optional, and can never be put away. Satan has ingeniously deceived believers into thinking that they have the option of taking time off from this profession. It is here that he is able to do his greatest damage.

To get a better understanding of this point, let's consider some characteristics of a soldier.

Characteristic 1: A soldier never forgets that he or she is at war.

A soldier never forgets that he or she is at war. One of the most deadly things that a soldier can do is to forget that he or she is engaged in a battle. When Gideon was narrowing his army for God, one of the things he observed was the way the soldiers drank water from the brook. The soldiers who were selected were alert; the soldiers who were careless were not selected.

Characteristic 2: A soldier must be disciplined.

The word "disciple" simply means "disciplined one." This root word of "discipline" means "one who exercises self control." It means to deny one's self at the cost of doing what's necessary or most important. Jesus said, **"Whoever wants to be my disciple must deny themselves and take up their cross and follow me."** (Matthew 16:24) I believe that one of the greatest quantum leaps that you can make is in the area of discipline. Satan's main strategy is to bank on believers being addicted to pleasure and ease. Yet, he is no match for a Christian with a made up mind to do whatever is necessary to win.

Characteristic 3: A soldier is familiar with his or her weaponry.

Do you know how to use the weapons that are in your arsenal? One of the tragic mistakes I see believers make is to try to use carnal weapons in a spiritual battle. You cannot revert back to the world's strategies to win this battle. "The weapons we fight with are not the weapons of the world. On the contrary, they have divine power to demolish strongholds." (II Corinthians 10:4) We must use God's weapons His way. His most potent weapon is love.

Characteristic 4: A soldier realizes that it is not about them. It is all about the team.

One of the first things a soldier must learn to do is to be selfless. In order for a platoon to operate successfully in a mission, it must operate as a single unit. In order to achieve victory, unity is vital. A soldier must always think of not only what is best for them individually, but what's best for the team. When they synergize and synchronize, they cannot be defeated. A team or platoon can be the workforce of a multinational corporation, a group of employees at a manufacturing plant, staff members at a non-profit organization, leaders in a ministry at church, or siblings in a family – any group of people working together to achieve a common goal, no matter how big or small.

Characteristic 5: A soldier has a victor's mentality vs. a victim's mentality.

In order to win, you must first believe that you can. You must take on a mentality of engagement, rather than passivity. You must realize that when you enlisted, you understood that there would be combat. Engage! Am I saying that you should enjoy the fight? Not necessarily, but it wouldn't hurt. Think about anyone exceptional at their profession, and you will usually find that they enjoy it. One of my personal heroes is Muhammad Ali. I believe that he is, without question, the greatest heavyweight boxing champion of all time. One of the things that made him so great was that he loved to fight. As a result, when he was in the ring, he had no equal. General George Patton loved battle, and Michael Jordan loved to play basketball. Joe Montana loved to play football, and Mother Teresa loved people. All of these great figures shared one important ingredient: a victor's mentality! They expected to win! One of the worst things that you can do as a soldier is to develop a victim's mentality.

Now let me pause here and say that I definitely understand that bad things will happen to you in life. You will likely face hurts, wrongs, and trials in your lifetime that will be unfair. Yet we must remember what Paul says in **Romans 8:37: "No, in all these things we are more than conquerors through him who loved us."** God gets no glory in hearing someone complain about hard it is to be a Christian. Rather, let rather our anthem always be **Philippians 4:13: "I have strength for all things in Christ Who empowers me (I am ready for anything and equal to anything through Him Who infuses inner strength into me; I am sufficient in Christ's sufficiency). (AMP**

Characteristic 6: A soldier studies their battle strategy at all times.

You have at your disposal the greatest battle strategy known to humankind called the Bible. In it contains every solution to every problem that your enemy, Satan, can throw at you. In this battle manual, you can know the mind of God and tap into God's thoughts. Study it daily. By successfully following the plans in this manual, you become invincible! Don't leave home without it.

Characteristic 7: A soldier realizes that they are not led by their emotions, but by their orders.

One of the crucial truths that a soldier learns is this one: "You must follow your orders, regardless of how you feel." In fact, the first thing a commander does is to ensure that the soldier understands the mission. Upon accepting it, the soldier agrees to all of the dangers, terms, and details that come with it. Have you ever wondered what would happen if we neglected to do everything we didn't feel like doing? What would have happened if Dr. Martin Luther King, Jr. had decided not to stand up for civil rights? What would have happened if Mohandas Gandhi had refused to stand up against the injustices in India, or if Mother Teresa had refused to go to Calcutta? I venture to say that history would have been much different

I do not want in any way to suggest that this will be easy. I can certainly understand and appreciate that this may require a change in mindset. As a child of God, there is limitless greatness in you. The Bible has made one thing clear about you as the offspring of God, and it is this: You are greater than your feelings! A soldier realizes that sometimes, you must do what you have to do. You may not enjoy the sacrifice now, but when you pay the price up front, regardless of the pain, you will enjoy the harvest later.

It is only when we understand the true concept of being a soldier that we are truly ready for victory. Just as one cannot lay down the responsibility of being a soldier in times of war, one cannot ignore the calling to be a soldier in a life of war – spiritual war. We are soldiers on the battlefield for God, and God has given us the weapons for victory.

Introduction

Mass production is God's idea. One of the great things that I love about God is His productive nature. In fact, before placing Adam and Eve in the Garden of Eden, He gave them an awesome assignment. What was this mighty task He laid before them? Mass production: the ability to produce greatly and perpetually in any situation. It was this concept of mass production, made famous by Henry Ford, which revolutionized our world. Though Ford was not the inventor of the automobile, he would become the face of it. His vision of mass-producing the motor car enabled the average American citizen who needed a car to own one. This concept revolutionized not only America, but changed the world as we know it. Because Ford had the foresight to think beyond himself, he became famously wealthy and served humankind as well.

In like manner, God is concerned with the whole of humankind being served. Though mass production was made famous by Ford, it was not a Ford original. The idea actually originated with God. **Genesis 1:28** records it this way: **"God blessed them and said to them, `Be fruitful and increase in number; fill the earth and subdue it. Rule over the fish in the sea and the birds in the sky and over every living creature that moves on the ground.'"** As I examine this passage of scripture, I must note the following. Before any instructions were given to Adam and Eve to mass produce, they were given something that would guarantee their success. They were given a key ingredient that would give them perpetual productivity, no matter what the environment. What was this ingredient? It was the blessing of God. God blessed them. The word "bless" means to empower to prosper and excel. God not only gave them the instructions and the authority, God gave them the power as well. That power is still available today. Though much has changed since the Garden of Eden, God's plan for mass production is still alive and well.

Now, let's fast forward to the twenty-first century American workforce. Today, we face perhaps the greatest downturn in our nation's economy since the Great Depression. According to a study conducted by the Conference Board in 2008, and reported online by the Huffington Post in 2010, workforce dissatisfaction is at an all-time low. At this time, only 45% of American employees enjoy their work, down from 61% in 1987. A nation once known for its prosperity has become the world's greatest debtor nation. Large corporations are either collapsing or downsizing. As a result of these trends, the morale of our workforce has been damaged greatly. The faith in God, inspiration, optimism, and can-do spirit that once characterized America has been replaced by doubt, fear, and skepticism.

As a corporate trainer, I have been blessed with the great opportunity to work with both American and international workforces. I have traveled to many states, presenting training to all types of companies. The companies range from universities, to Fortune 500 companies, to the United States Armed Forces. I have had the great pleasure of meeting and talking with employees. I have heard all types of stories, but most of all I have heard complaints. The complaints range from trouble dealing with difficult bosses, to a lack of leadership, from a lack of fairness, to fears over job security, from not enough income, to the inability to give one's input. What's worse is that many feel God has abandoned them, that He is not listening, and that bad people seem to prosper. They see the promises, but no manifestation. It is as if God has left them here to fight with no weapons.

But is this true? Is God here? Has God left you weapons with which to fight? The answer is a resounding YES! Not only has God left you weapons, but mighty weapons. **II Corinthians 10:4** says, **"For the weapons of our warfare are not carnal, but mighty through God" (KJV)**

If any of these scenarios sound familiar to you, congratulations on your decision to own this book. Welcome to a twenty-one day discovery of your new victorious destiny in Christ! In this powerful book, we will explore twenty-one weapons of power and production. Each weapon launched unlocks a powerful principle designed to attack the enemy. Collectively, they form an unbeatable arsenal that will catapult you from failure to supernatural productivity and success in God. In this book you will learn how to guard your mind from unproductive thoughts and habits. You will discover the tremendous productivity that comes from living and operating in wisdom. You will also learn the power of changing your mindset from that of a grasshopper to the spiritual giant God created you to be. Through the reading and application of this book, you will not merely survive, but thrive!

Why 21 Days?

Twenty-one is a significant number for a few reasons. Studies show that it takes approximately twenty-one days to form a new habit. In the book of Daniel, the prophet prayed fervently for twenty-one days before the prince of Persia relented to God's will. The archangel Michael told Daniel that God had been listening to Daniel's prayers from day one, but that God's time is not our own. The premise, both naturally and spiritually, is that if you consciously apply a principle to your life each day, you will see a marked change. The goal of this book is to change your life. Internalize these principles in your heart to experience true life transformation.

Why This Book?

In addition to the earlier statistics about workforce inspiration, there were equally disturbing discoveries regarding workforce health. Simply put, people are dreading their jobs and their work to the detriment of their health. Another article published online by CNN, entitled "Monday Mornings Bad for Your Health," revealed more shocking information. According to this study, due to the dread of Mondays, more heart attacks took place on that day than any other day of the week. Similarly, earlier research revealed another startling statistic. More suicides occurred on Monday than any other day of the week. This is a literal fulfillment of what Jesus spoke of in **Luke 21:26** when he said, **"People will faint from terror, apprehensive of what is coming on the world, for the heavenly bodies will be shaken."**

Such failures of heart are not God's will. Your life was not intended to be lived this way. God intended for you to live vigorously, courageously, and productively. God has a wonderful plan for your life regarding your work. **Ecclesiastes 3:12-13** declares this great statement concerning your work: **"I know that there is nothing better for people than to be happy and to do good while they live. That each of them may eat and drink, and find satisfaction in all their toil—this is the gift of God."** In this passage, we see a powerful truth:

God wants you to be joyful and take pleasure in your toil. God even goes on to say that work is God's gift to us.

Far too often we see work not as a gift, but as a "four letter word." Many people today perceive work to be a curse. However, if you recognize work for what it truly is, you will realize that you are laboring under a blessing, and not a curse. The purpose of this book is to bring the joy, fulfillment, and productivity back into your job, your career, and your life. After twenty-one days, you will have received true inspiration that improves your work-life, and your total life, as well. Jesus said in **John 10:10 "The thief comes only to steal and kill and destroy; I have come that they may have life, and have it to the full."** Learn to incorporate God's offer of abundance in all areas of your life. In this book, you will discover how to get meaning, joy, and fulfillment from your work by being productive. You will also discover how to rekindle and regain the joy that so many have lost. Once this twenty-one day journey is complete, you will discover the gift that God created work to be to you, not only work performed as a job, but your life's work – the kind of work for which God created you to do.

Who will benefit from this book?

Many will benefit from this book. This book is written for:

- Frustrated employees who lack zest, joy, and confidence, or a desire to put forth their best effort.

- People who are void of passion and purpose in their current profession, desiring not just a job, but an adventure.

- The employees who desire to go into business for themselves, but who need to grasp the vital principles of success first.

- Those who are in need of inspiration and faith.

- Those who have grown weary and forgotten how clearly God sees every individual.

- Leaders and entrepreneurs who desire to truly inspire their employees to do their best work and give their best effort.

- Those who want to learn how to solicit true commitment to their corporate mission statements in order to yield great performance.

- Teachers and parents who crave perspective and insight into how to inspire young people to be true Godly leaders.

- Married couples desiring to recalibrate and refocus their marriage and learn to walk in love toward one another.

- Employees shackled by cynicism as a result of the duplicity of leadership.

This book was written for anyone who wants to fulfill their destiny in God and maximize their God-ordained potential.

How To Use This Book

I wrote this book to give readers a twenty-one day guide to assist them in adding Godly productivity and fulfillment to their lives. As a result, each chapter has been divided into three parts: Inspiration, Information, and Application.

Inspiration- Each chapter is designed to inspire you as you discover your new weapon by exploring its power and examining the best strategy to make the weapon effective. Take time to reflect on what you have read.

Information- At the end of each chapter, I have provided seven recommendations, questions, or keys to assist you in using the weapon properly. Like any weapon, if it not used properly, it could be destructive, rather than productive.

Application- Of the suggestions mentioned, I recommend that you choose the one that works best for you, or is to your liking, and act on it. I have found that people tend to act on things that they like. Make a decision to act on it within the next twenty-one days. Remember, it only takes approximately twenty-one days to form a new habit. Once you begin to act on it consistently, it becomes habit-forming. Many of you may be asking, "Why only list one thing to act on?" I recommend one thing because sometimes we overwhelm ourselves and over commit, only to result in broken promises. By choosing to act on at least one thing, you are less likely to overwhelm yourself. Sometimes, even the smallest actions can yield the greatest results. Am I implying that you must choose the recommendations that I have provided to you? Absolutely not. You may have suggestions that are better than the ones provided. Feel free to use your own, if necessary. I am not suggesting, however, that you do nothing

Your decision to read this book is a great step in the right direction to achieve mass production with God. Your life will never be the same again. So strap in, saddle up, and lock and load, as together we prepare to launch Weapons of Mass Production.

Chapter 1

Weapons of Mass Destruction

*"There are seeds of self destruction in all of us
that will only bear unhappiness if allowed to grow."*
-Dorothea Brand

*"There is a way that seems right in a man's eyes,
but the end thereof leads to destruction."*
-Proverbs 14:12

On September 11, 2001 our nation experienced perhaps its greatest tragedy. On that fateful morning millions watched as terrorists flew two high-jacked planes into both of the World Trade Center towers in New York. This horrible day of tragedy will forever live in the hearts of Americans. It was later discovered that the attack was devised by international terrorist Osama Bin Laden. Shortly afterwards, our government supposedly discovered some alarming news: Iraq, under the direction of Saddam Hussein, had dangerous nuclear and biological weapons. These weapons, referred to as "Weapons of Mass Destruction," had the capability of killing and injuring thousands, if not millions, of people. Our nation reported that intelligence existed to indicate that Iraq had these weapons in hiding. As the United Nations met regarding this suspicion, the world watched anxiously. Still reeling from the tragedy of 9-11, our nation was gripped with fear at the prospect of yet another attack. Subsequently, we went to war with Iraq, and we overthrew the brutal dictatorship of Saddam Hussein. We easily defeated that nation, but ironically, we never found the "Weapons of Mass Destruction." It was later discovered, after careful search, that there were no weapons. By then, "Weapons of Mass Destruction" had become a household term, although no weapons were actually found by our government.

Let me share some startling facts. Not only did the weapons exist, they are still in existence today. They were actually discovered over 2000 years ago. Although they were never discovered in Iraq, they were discovered in the Middle East. This enemy who possesses these weapons is alive and well today. He not only seeks to destroy America, but all of humankind. These weapons, however, are far more powerful and destructive than any nuclear bomb. What makes them so powerful is that they don't attack us from the outside, but from within. They attack the heart. They attack our productivity. Who is this enemy and what is his weapon? The enemy is Satan. His strategy is simple: He seeks to kill, to steal, and to destroy. He does this by attacking the hearts and minds of men and women, by attacking from the inside. He can inflict far worse damage than any "man-made" weapon as he tears at the very fabric of our souls. One's lack of productivity is evidence of a soul under attack.

Who discovered these weapons and where were they discovered? Jesus Christ discovered them over two thousand years ago in Israel and Judea. To get a better understanding of these weapons, and how the enemy works, let's examine the words of Jesus. In the Gospel of Mark, Jesus is confronted by the Pharisees. The Pharisees were known for being analytical, but missing the big picture. In other words, they majored on the minors, and minored on the majors. As they confront him they ask him why he allows his disciples to eat with unwashed hands. Jesus gives them this reply in **Mark 7:14-23**

Again Jesus called the crowd to him and said, "Listen to me, everyone, and understand this. 15 Nothing outside a person can defile them by going into them. Rather, it is what comes out of a person that defiles them." [16]]

17 **After he had left the crowd and entered the house, his disciples asked him about this parable.** 18 **"Are you so dull?" he asked. "Don't you see that nothing that enters a person from the outside can defile them?** 19 **For it doesn't go into their heart but into their stomach, and then out of the body." (In saying this, Jesus declared all foods clean.)**

[20] He went on: **"What comes out of a person is what defiles them.** [21] **For it is from within, out of a person's heart, that evil thoughts come—sexual immorality, theft, murder,** [22] **adultery, greed, malice, deceit, lewdness, envy, slander, arrogance and folly.** [23] **All these evils come from inside and defile a person.**

In this passage, Jesus identifies and locates the Weapons of Mass Destruction as those bad things that infiltrate the heart. They can be wrong attitudes, anger, or offenses. They may also be prejudices, blame, selfishness, or pride. These dangerous weapons cause us to be defiled, thus paralyzing our productivity.

To further illustrate this point, consider the fate of the great steamship, the Titanic. The tragedy of the Titanic greatly illustrates the phrase, "the tip of the iceberg." The part of the iceberg that you can see above water – the tip – represents in many instances, only 5% of its actual size. This great ship, which was capable of carrying over 3000 passengers, was supposedly indestructible and unsinkable. Reportedly, some declared, "Even God himself couldn't sink the Titanic." Yet, on April 15, 1912, the colossal ship struck an iceberg off the coast of Newfoundland and sank. The iceberg shredded the underbelly of the ship like paper, causing it to sink in approximately two hours. Like the Titanic, when we look at only the surface issues in our lives, while failing to look underwater, we are certain to sink

The Heart

God loved humankind so much that God placed a piece of Himself in every one of us. Where did God place this piece? In our hearts. In fact, **Ecclesiastes 3:11** reads, **"He has made everything beautiful in its time. He has also set eternity in the human heart; yet no one can fathom what God has done from beginning to end."** The heart is now, and always has been the center of men and women. It is the heart that sustains life by pumping blood to the other parts of the body. So much so, that when poison gets in the blood stream, it goes straight to the heart. The heart pumps life through the blood, and they both work hand in hand. It is the heart that is in the center of the body. It is the heart that has to keep beating in order for human beings to live. When a hunter is hunting for his or her prey, it is vital that he or she aim for the heart in order to bring a large animal down. Even the writers of fiction and horror understand this concept. Have you ever seen a vampire movie? How does the hero kill the vampire? You guessed it! It is by driving a wooden stake through the creature's heart.

In similar fashion, the enemy attempts to get to the heart of the believer and defile it. He knows that if he can defile the heart, the rest of the body is sure to die. King Solomon, considered the wisest man who ever lived, understood this well. Perhaps that's why he gives such vital instruction concerning the heart in the book of Proverbs. In **Proverbs 4:23**, King Solomon says, **"Keep thy heart with all diligence; for out of it are the issues of life."** Why did he write the "issues of life"? What are they? I think that we would all agree that these are legitimate questions.

We are either one of two things, dead or alive. Jesus himself said, **"I am come that ye might have life, and life more abundantly." John 10:10** So what are the issues of life? The issues of life are those things in our lives that determine our success or failure. The issues of life are those weighty matters that empower us to succeed or fail in life with God. These vital issues are what we must protect and keep alive.

I hope by now you are beginning to get the picture. The entire battle is over the heart. Now what do we mean when we refer to the heart? No, I'm not speaking of the great organ in your chest cavity that keeps you alive. I am speaking of the true center of your being. I am referring to your mind, your will, and your emotions. I am referring to your desires. When Satan is allowed to attack the heart, and dominate the mind, the will, and the emotions, destruction is inevitable. Although his ultimate goal for us is death, Satan will allow us to simply to go in circles, never making progress, for a time. In many instances this means a slow death. God did not intend for us to live this way. We were made to be victorious in Christ Jesus. Henry David Thoreau said, "There are a thousand hacking at the branches of evil to one hacking at the root." When you monitor your heart condition and address the underlying issues of your heart, you attack Satan at his weakest point. In dealing with the heart, you are addressing the root of the problem, rather than merely the symptoms. Whenever you only look at the symptoms of an issue without addressing the root, destruction is inevitable.

It's Time to Reclaim Your Heart

In **Luke 21:26** Jesus said that in the last days, men's (human being's) hearts would **"fail them for fear."** If our society today is characterized by anything, it is fear. Satan has so loaded down the hearts of people that their hearts are being governed by fear instead of faith. This spirit did not come from God, and therefore, God can't operate the way He wants in your life. This is not the life that God intended for you to live. God gave you a life of abundance and productivity. **II Timothy 1:8** reads: **"For God hath not given us a spirit of fear, but of power, and love, and of a sound mind."** A sound mind is a mind that is built up in faith, trusting that God will do what He said. It is time to get your heart back friend. Jesus said these powerful words in **John 14:27 "Peace I leave with you; my peace I give you. I do not give to you as the world gives. Do not let your hearts be troubled and do not be afraid."** Those words are as true today as they were then. Satan walks about as a roaring lion seeking whom he may devour. Make the determination that he will not devour you! When he seeks to devour you, let him get a mouthful of steel!

The Two Laws Governing the Heart

There are two main laws that will govern the heart, the Law of Sin and Death and the Law of Life in Christ Jesus. The rewards of one law lead to the abundant life that God has prepared for us, and the punishment of the other leads to death, non-productivity, and destruction. The Law of Life in Christ Jesus is the path of love and faith, resulting in productivity and abundance. The Law of Sin and Death is the path of fear and doubt, resulting in stagnation, lack, and excuses. To get a better understanding of these two laws, let's examine **Galatians 5:19 and 22.**

The Law of Sin and Death

"Now the works of the flesh are manifest, which are these: Adultery, fornication, uncleanness, lasciviousness, idolatry, witchcraft, hatred, variance, emulations, wrath, strife, seditions, heresies, envyings, murders, drunkenness, reveling, and such like:

of the which I tell you before, as I have told you in time past, that they which do such things shall not inherit the Kingdom of God." Galatians 5:19

This scripture illustrates the essence of the weapons of mass destruction. You will notice that it says that they which practice such things shall not inherit the Kingdom of God. Paul is not referring to heaven, but God's way or system of doing business. In short, he is saying that those that practice these things won't enjoy the system of blessing that God has designed for His people. Notice that there are seventeen descriptions which characterize the works of the flesh. One of Satan's strategies has been to throw so much at believers that they will spend their lives off balance and on the defensive. As long as we have a mentality of defense, we won't concentrate on offense. As long as we are focused on survival, we will never think about revival. It is time for us to carry the fight to Satan and attack! By cutting off the works of the flesh, we are closing the entryway for him to attack our hearts and our productivity.

The Law of Love and Life in Christ Jesus-The True Power

"But the fruit of the Spirit is love, joy, peace, longsuffering, gentleness, goodness, faith, meekness, temperance: against such there is no law." Galatians 5:22

This passage of scripture imparts an important truth. The passage ends by declaring, **"against such there is no law."** There is nothing that can defend against this fruit. By operating and cultivating these qualities in our hearts, we literally rise above the Law of Sin and Death. Satan makes a tragic mistake here. Because there are only nine characteristics, as opposed to seventeen, he assumes that his seventeen devices are more powerful. However, he does not understand an important truth: The Spirit of Light is much more powerful than the Spirit of Darkness. How do we attack Satan? How can we back him up on his heels? We can do so by exercising the love of God through the Fruit of the Spirit. Paul writes something powerful at the end of I Corinthians 13: **"Love never fails."** Like the majestic eagle, we can fly higher than the turbulence we encounter. Love is the way to get there. Many of us have been lulled to sleep by Satan's devices and craftiness. We have spent so much time defending that we have forgotten to attack. Satan's worst nightmare is for God's people to attack him, not merely defend against him, but to storm the very gates of Hell! When we spend time developing the fruit of the Spirit, we are mounting an all- out offensive that Satan cannot defend! It is time that we quit settling for field goals and score some touchdowns!

Listen to this great admonition from our Commander and Chief in **Luke 10:19: "I have given you authority to trample on snakes and scorpions and to overcome all the power of the enemy; nothing will harm you."** Now is the time for us to use the power that we have been given! No longer do you have to fear. You have been given the permission, the weapons, and the authority by God to win. The great news is that the outcome of the fight has already been determined! Your success is guaranteed. The only question that remains is this: Are you ready to attack? If so, let's go up at once and possess the land! Hallelujah!

Weapons of Mass Production

Chapter 2

Put God Things First

"The circumference of life cannot be measured until the center has been set."

-Benjamin E. Mays

"But seek ye first the Kingdom of God and all His righteousness, and all these things will be added unto you."

-Matthew 6:33

Weapon #1: Put God Things First

Why It Is Powerful

It all starts with God.

One of my favorite books of all time is the national bestseller, *The 7 Habits of Highly Effective People,* by Dr. Stephen R. Covey. This tremendous book been dominated bestseller lists, sold over 15 million copies, and been translated into dozens of languages for a reason. In his insightful book, Dr. Covey expounds on seven powerful habits of effectiveness. I really appreciate this book because it clarifies the difference between being busy and being truly effective. Habit # 2 is "Put First Things First." In other words, you must prioritize if you want to be effective. You must decide on the tasks that are most important and tackle them first.

This concept has become one of the most important and powerful business principles. It is taught in corporations worldwide through time management or leadership seminars. If you visit any successful corporation, it is highly likely you will see this great concept posted somewhere. Covey teaches that the consequences of ignoring the important tasks lead to ineffectiveness, frustration, and chaos. First things include meetings, budgeting, coaching, and team building. Nevertheless, there is one problem with the direction that most businesses and employees have taken. They have left God out the category of first things. They have used logical, analytical reasoning, and bottom-line based strategies instead of Biblical ones. Without God as the basis for your success, you are destined to fail.

Strategy for Victory

Genesis begins with four very important words: "In the beginning God..." If we were to stop reading the Bible here, we would have enough wisdom to last a lifetime. You see God was there in the beginning, and God will be there at the end. God is the Alpha and Omega, the beginning and the end, all at the same time. God existed before time, created time, and stepped into time, sending His son to die for the sins of humankind. Unfortunately, humankind has an uncanny ability to have a short memory, and a tendency to attempt to reduce God to our state as human beings.

For instance, if I were to ask, "What is the first number in the numerical system?" Most people would probably answer by saying "One." However, in order to answer that question, it would be important to know the numerical system I am using. According to certain numerical systems, the answer would be "0," followed by "1." Do you get my point? God occupies that space that is at zero. Just as zero comes before 1, God came before time, and thus comes before first things. Everything was made by God.

President Harry S. Truman coined the phrase, "The buck stops here." Although this is a common, often used phrase, President Truman was wrong. You see the buck stops with God. Not only did God create the buck, but if God is not the foundation of your organization, you will find it much harder to make any "bucks."

Savvy, highly intelligent people occupy many places of leadership and influence in the world, and many people look to them for guidance and wisdom. They know all the right answers and phrases.

They have learned the right language, protocol, and customs. Yet, they have missed that most important concept, a relationship with God. I don't mean the gods of power, television, or whatever you call god. I am speaking of the true and living God that cares about every aspect of your life, including your success. Don't let this happen to you. Don't miss having a relationship with God.

Joseph knew that in order for him to be successful, he had to have total dependence on the only true author of our success and wealth, Jehovah. Pharaoh's magicians and astrologers may have known all of the cheap tricks, but there was only one man in the land that could give the true interpretation of Pharaoh's dreams. Are you that person in your company? Can you interpret the vision in order to accomplish great things?

The secret to Joseph's success can be found in **Deuteronomy 8:18**. It reads: **"But thou shalt remember the LORD thy God: for it is he that giveth thee power to get wealth, that he may establish his covenant which he swore unto thy fathers, as it is this day."**

Implementing the Strategy

7 Tactics to Put God Things First on the Battlefield

1. **Thank God for everything He has done for you.**
   Acknowledge Him in all of your ways, giving Him the glory for all of your accomplishments.

2. **Spend time alone with God in prayer.** God is a jealous God. God desires to have fellowship with you. God wants to hear your thoughts, and wants to talk with you. Set aside time each day to fellowship with Him. Let nothing interrupt that time, and watch how your life begins to change.

3. **Study your Bible daily.** The Bible is your manual for life. It is a success guide for Godly living. It contains the very "Words of Life," as Peter said. When we know God's word, we will know God's ways. Make the Word your final authority in life.

4. **Attend church and Bible Study weekly.** Being taught the word of God is vital to your success. We have a need to be edified and taught. Find a Bible-believing church, if you don't have one, and make it a point to try to get in two teachings per week.

Do you have to do this? No, but remember that those who are successful are usually willing to go the extra mile when unsuccessful people are not.

5. **Give your testimony!** Revelation 12:11 says, "They overcame by the blood of the lamb and the word of their testimony." Your testimony is one of the most powerful things you possess. Not only does it bless you, but it is designed to build faith in others. A testimony demonstrates that you are not ashamed of the Gospel. History is God's story. People are waiting to hear yours.

6. **Respect and honor your family.** The family unit is very important to God. There will be constant challenges to prevent you from spending time with your family. Ensure that you don't compromise your principles where your family is concerned. One of the ways that you honor God is by honoring your spouse and children.

7. **Walk in love.** One of the greatest ways to put God first is through loving God's people. This is perhaps the greatest challenge for most. Walking in love means blessing people by showing genuine kindness and selflessness toward others. It is choosing to forgive, when people don't deserve it or appreciate it. When we do this, it opens God's heart toward us.

When we remember to put God first in all of our affairs, God will ensure that we are placed first in the affairs of the world.

Now, you have the weapon. How are you going to use it?

Victory is mine! In the next 7 days, I will act on the following in order to Put God Things First:

_____

_____

_____

_____

Chapter 3

Take Time to Pray

"Prayer is where the action is."
-John Wesley

"Pray without ceasing."
I Thessalonians 5:17

Weapon #2: Take Time to Pray

Why It Is Powerful

What a wonderful and powerful privilege it is to have the powerful, yet often underrated, weapon of prayer. **Luke 18:1** says, **"Then Jesus told his disciples a parable to show them that they should always pray and not give up."** I Thessalonians 5:17 says that we should **"Pray without ceasing."** As we read these scriptures we realize that prayer should not be an activity, but a lifestyle.

WPM Q&A:

Q: If you were a championship boxer, facing a devastatingly dangerous opponent, would you train? Would you go through the necessary preparation and conditioning to win?

A: Yes. No matter how many films you have watched of your opponent or how much knowledge you possess, training is crucial for victory. A fighter entering the ring without training is what it's like when you go to into the workforce without praying.

We do not see victory in the workforce because we have forgotten a very important fact: We are at war! This is a battle, and we have not given it the proper attention required to win. Why do you suppose Paul urges us in **Ephesians 6:11** to **"put on the whole armor of God that ye may be able to withstand the wiles of the devil?"** You are facing a devastating opponent. His name is Satan, and he desires not only to beat you, but to destroy you, to kill you. Training is not optional.

It is absolutely ridiculous to think that one can be successful against an opponent like Satan without prayer. You have been given tremendous weapons of power, but they are useless if you don't use them and fight. You cannot defeat Satan with a passive, defensive, mindset regarding prayer. Prayer must not be a last resort, but a first resort! Prayer changes the equation and evens the score. Through the power of prayer, common people achieve uncommon results. Through prayer, you can part the Red Sea and outrun a chariot. With the weapon of prayer, you can become a king and defeat an army many times your size. Through prayer an orphan girl can become a queen and save her nation from annihilation. It is through prayer that you create the mindset of becoming a true son or daughter of God through Christ, tapping into an infinite wealth of wisdom In order for you to become productive in God, it is vital that you take time to pray.

Sadly enough in our society today, few truly understand the power, privilege, and potential of prayer. One of the main reasons that people are not experiencing breakthrough and success in the workplace is because of a lack of prayer. The Word says that **"in your presence there is fullness of joy, and at your right hand there are pleasures forevermore."** There's just one problem. We want the fullness of joy and the pleasures forevermore, but we do not want to come into His presence to get them. To quote my pastor, Dr. Creflo Dollar, "every problem in life is a prayer problem." In many cases, people tend to look at prayer as a last resort, having little or no power. How often have you had a friend in a dire situation say, "All I know to do is pray." It is as if they don't believe that God will hear them or even answer them. Why is this? It is because people have lost a Biblical perspective. They have allowed the affairs of this world to choke the life out of their faith in both God's willingness and ability to deliver them. They have magnified things, people, and circumstances over their God.

In regard to prayer Martin Luther stated, "Prayer is not overcoming God's reluctance, but laying hold of His willingness." So many of us have lost the determination to lay hold of God's willingness. You cannot defeat Satan with a passive, defensive, mindset regarding prayer. Prayer must not be a last resort, but a first resort! William Cowper asserted, "Satan trembles when he sees the weakest Christian on his knees." We must realize that, in order to win this battle, we must take a violent and offensive attitude toward the devil! Jesus delivers these great words regarding battle in **Matthew 11:12**, saying, **"From the days of John the Baptist until now, the kingdom of heaven suffers violence, and the violent take it by force."** We cannot postpone a match that has already been set. The fight is on, and our victory is imminent! We have forgotten the great things that happen when men and women pray.

To illustrate further, let's examine some of the results of people who prayed:

- Through prayer and fasting, Esther saved her nation from annihilation.

- Through prayer, Daniel was delivered from a lion's den unharmed.

- Through prayer, Joseph became the Prime Minister of Egypt.

- Because of Hezekiah's prayer, the Lord delivered Israel, killing 185, 000 Assyrians.

- Through Hezekiah' prayer, God adds 15 years to Hezekiah's life, after pronouncing death.

- Through Elijah's prayer, God sent fire and Elijah slew the prophets of Baal.

- Because of Gideon's prayer, an army of only 300 men defeats and army of 135,000 Midianites.

What an amazing list of accomplishments through the power of prayer! If God can achieve these feats, what makes you think that He can't move the heart of a difficult boss? What makes you believe that God won't move on your behalf regarding the promotion for which you are being considered? God loves you, friend, and wants to see you prosper

Strategy for Victory

Action 1: Utilize Your God-given Authority

I once heard an attorney say, "If you don't know your rights, you have no rights." In other words, the law is beneficial only to those who know it. I have an important question to ask you. Do you know your rights as a son and daughter of God? If you don't, then you are likely giving away, not only your rights to Satan, but your abundant life as well. You have been given both the power and the authority to pummel the devil whenever you feel like it! The problem is, you will only utilize what you know. Consider these great words that Jesus left with us in **Luke 10:19: "Behold, I give unto you power to tread over serpents and scorpions, and over all the power of the enemy, and nothing shall by any means hurt you."** Jesus starts this statement by saying "Behold!" In other words, whatever you do, don't miss this point! Jesus proclaims that not only do you have power to tread over serpents and scorpions, but over ALL the power of the enemy! Hallelujah! He doesn't stop there. He says something else that most people miss, and it is this: **"And nothing shall by any means hurt you!"**

Action 2: Start Your Day with Morning Prayer

If I could only recommend one thing that would make the largest quantum leap in your work performance, it would be Morning Prayer. One of the most potent strategies of the enemy is to jam your communication before you even start your morning. His primary goal is to distract you from praying. Have you ever noticed the distractions that come at you first thing in the morning? When you make the decision to pray, you are likely to receive everything from a phone call to a knock at the door. You may think these are coincidences, but they are not. They are all by design, because the Devil knows when you fall on your knees and pray, he trembles in fear. I have found that there are things that are significant about Morning Prayer. Some may say, "I'm not a morning person." If I offered to give you a million dollars to wake up at 5:00 a.m., could you become a "morning person?" I think I know the answer. You probably answered, "Yes." Is it possible that rather than being incapable of being a morning person, you have just never decided to become a morning person?

One of the greatest examples of the results of Morning Prayer is Joseph. Now many of you are probably scratching your heads. You are probably asking the question, "How do you know that Joseph prayed in the morning, or even at all, since nowhere in the Bible does it say he prayed?" That's a very good question. There are a couple of reasons. The first reason are the results that he received. The Bible says this in Genesis regarding Joseph's life, **"And the Lord was with Joseph."** Do you think that there is any way that Joseph could have the Lord with him without being diligent about prayer?

The second reason we know that Joseph was a man of Morning Prayer is because of who his father was. You remember his father, Jacob? You know the one who wrestled with the angel of the Lord until the wee hours of the morning? The same man who said that he wouldn't release him until God blessed him? I believe that Jacob learned something powerful about the morning that he never forgot. It was after that morning that he would never be the same again. Though he would walk with a limp from that time on, there is no amount of money that he would have taken in exchange for that experience. Jacob poured everything he had into Joseph. Because of Joseph's father, we do not have to wonder whether Joseph prayed.

When we make the decision to charge our days with power-packed, Morning Prayer with God, we will never be the same again, either. When you plug into God's power as your first act of the day, you carry a charge and current with you to work that will literally change the atmosphere and the encounters you have with people throughout the day.

Morning Prayer is powerful for a number of reasons.

First, it is literally waking up to God. When God is the first person you speak with without distraction, it pleases Him. You are making God a priority and inviting Him to speak to you regarding your day.

Second, it is a sacrifice to get up early, and God knows it. In doing so, you are giving Him the best part of your day. In Genesis, it says that God met Adam in the "cool of the day." I believe that it was in the morning because that is when it is the coolest.

Third, you mount an early offensive against Satan. He has been up all night attempting to attack you. Now, some people may say, "I don't start my prayer until about 11 o'clock." By then the enemy has already laid out ambushes and sent reinforcements against you. Have you ever noticed how you feel when you don't pray? You don't seem to have that edge. Why is that? Deep down inside you didn't sacrifice to give God your best. You know that you are lacking a core component.

Fourth, morning prayer is unique and powerful, because it is a recreation of creation all over again. You see, it was out of the darkness that God said, "Let there be light!" When the new day breaks, it is a thing of beauty! Have you ever taken the time to notice the beauty and majesty of a sunrise? How can you possibly stay depressed when you are being engaged with God in His beauty?

Fifth and finally, when you get in God's presence before starting work, you carry God's glory to work with you! The same glory that Moses expressed on his face upon returning from Mount Sinai, you carry that into the marketplace. Glory to God!

Action 3: Welcome Solitude

In this day of high-tech and interactive technology, solitude, has become something that many people shun. Whenever most people think of solitude, they tend to focus on loneliness or sadness. Unfortunately, many people today have no appreciation for solitude or serenity. They tend to regard it as some form of leprosy or a plague. However, solitude, properly understood, is a rare commodity from which great solutions are produced. As I discuss the importance of productivity, it is very important that I make a crucial point here: Anyone who ever did anything great for God, had to first have an appreciation for being alone with Him. Solitude is defined as: a separation from others or seclusion; singleness; loneliness; or wilderness. For these purposes, let's focus on the term: "a separation from others."

In order to consider the importance of separation from others, let's examine the most productive man who ever lived, our Lord Jesus. **Acts 10:38** says, **"How that God anointed Jesus Christ of Nazareth with the Holy Ghost and power, who went about doing good, and healing all that were oppressed of the devil."** The key word I would like to emphasize here is "all." Jesus healed them all! Talk about productivity! How would you like to have a 100% success ratio in your business? Let's examine Jesus' exploits in production.

What Did Jesus Do?

Jesus' Adventures in Production

- He turned water into wine at a wedding.

- He fed 5,000 men, women, and children with two fish and five loaves.

- He paid taxes out of a fish's mouth.

- On two occasions He had record-breaking success in the fishing industry.

- He raised Lazarus from the dead after 4 days in a tomb.

- He restored a Roman soldier's ear after it had been cut off.

- He walked on water and calmed a raging storm.

Wow! What an amazing list of accomplishments in productivity. Yet how many times in scripture do we read where it says, "And Jesus went to a solitary place to pray." No matter how many great exploits Jesus performed, He found time to be alone with His Father. He knew that the source of His power was time spent with God. Let's examine Jesus' pattern of productivity in a typical day.

1. He arose early while it was yet dark. (This wipes out about half of us.)

2. He started His day entering into God's presence and filling up His tank with God's love and power.

3. He went out and performed great exploits, healing the sick, performing miracles, and casting out devils.

4. He taught His disciples by demonstration.

5. He ate and fellowshipped.

6. He relaxed and slept.

7. He woke and repeated the process again. Just as Jesus could perform no miracles without solitude and time with God, neither can we. neither can we.

Implementing the Strategy

7 Tactics to Use Prayer on the Battlefield

1. Enter God's presence with thanksgiving and praise. Thank Him not only for what He's done, but for who He is.

2. Use the Blood of Jesus to enter into God's presence. The Bible tells us in Hebrews 10:19 "Having therefore, brethren, boldness to enter into the holiest by the blood of Jesus." Enter God's presence by thanking Him for what Jesus' blood purchased for you.

3. Make a place in your home where you meet God. By doing so, you are literally setting a place for God.

4. Always have a notepad to write down any instructions that God may give you or speak to you.

5. Listen. Don't feel like you always have to talk. Dialogue is two-way communication. Listen for what God may be saying to you

6. Pray according to the Word of God. Have your Bible available to refer to the scriptures as needed or led.

7. Seal your prayer by thanking God for answering you in accordance with Mark 11:24 "Therefore I tell you, whatever you ask for in prayer, believe that you have received it, and it will be yours."

It is very important that I mention an important point regarding prayer. Many believe that all you have to do is pray, and God takes care of the rest. Nothing could be farther from the truth! We must follow up our prayer with hard work. In fact, your hard work is an act of your faith. It is only after having prayed that you have the confidence to expect God to move because you are giving God something to work with.

Now, you have the weapon. How are you going to use it?

Victory is mine! In the next 7 days, I will act on the following in order to Take Time to Pray:

_____

_____

_____

_____

Chapter 4

Walk In Love

"Faith makes all things possible, love makes them easy."
-Unknown

"Love never fails"
I Corinthians 13:8

Weapon #3: Walk In Love

Why It Is Powerful

The one vital ingredient for unlimited productivity in God is the ever-enduring, never failing quality of love. Love is that great quality that Jesus spoke of and championed for most of His life. In fact, He said that it would be the earmark, or indication that we were His disciples. In I Corinthians, the Apostle Paul gives us the wonderful qualities of love. He talks about how love is patient and kind. He goes on to say that it seeks not its own and isn't puffed up or haughty. However, I think Paul's summation of love really says it all. In **I Corinthians 13:8** Paul simply and yet powerfully states, **"Love never fails."**

WMP Q&A:

Q: Have you been trying methods that have failed you time and time again? Have systems, techniques, or programs that you thought were rock-solid let you down? What about people? Have you ever placed your faith or confidence in someone, only to have them fail or disappoint you?

A: Chances are, if you are living, the answer is a resounding, "Yes." It is only the quality of love that will deliver every time.

Still not convinced? Consider what the Bible says about the power of love. To carefully examine love and the results that it produces, we would have to consider Love Himself, our Lord and savior, Jesus Christ. The Bible says that God is love. It goes on to say in **John 3:16** that **"God so loved the world that He gave His only begotten son."** You see God deposited everything that He was into Jesus. In other words, God, who is love, so loved the world, that He sent Love himself to redeem humankind! Jesus said this, "If you have seen me, you have seen the father." What He meant was that everything that was in the Father, was in Him. So if that was the case, then Jesus and His father were one.

Strategy for Victory

When our love is combined with diligence, persistence, and character, we will prosper in any recession and outlast any hardship.

WMP Q&A:

Q: Many of you are probably asking the same questions right now such as, "What does love have to do with my being productive?" or "How is love going to help me prosper and excel in my job, or in my business?"

A: These are both great questions. By cultivating, demonstrating, and walking in the spirit of love in our lives, we walk in the same type of productivity in which Jesus walked. We bring life and vitality to our jobs, creating a level that confounds our wisdom and transcends our natural ability or intellect.

Many times we meet people of character who always produce uncommon results. They are living for God. When things don't go their way, they don't become bitter. Instead, they seem to love even more when challenged. Yet, they consistently exhibit productivity that nobody seems to understand, sometimes accounting for the work of two or three people.

These people have cultivated and developed the spirit of love, and it is manifesting in their lives outwardly. Cultivating the spirit of love means spending time, on purpose, developing yourself in love and patience. Make it your main priority to build this into your spirit through active practice, faith in, and study of God's word. I will not say that this development will be easy, because it won't be. It will take time, effort, focus, and persistence. Nothing worthwhile in life besides God's grace is ever easy to receive. However, like anything else you have learned to do well, it will get easier with practice.

Biblical Examples of the Strategy: Cultivating the Spirit of Love

To consider the absolute power of the effect of love on productivity and results, consider several people in the Bible and in history who possessed this great quality. The one thing that made them great and separated them from others was the spirit of love. Many people in our workforce today simply do not understand the importance of love. They've tried every scheme known to humankind, and yet they continue to perform at sub-par levels. They blame people, conditions, the government, and even systems for their lack of results. However, they never seem to accept the responsibility themselves. Am I saying that many of them have not been treated unfairly? Not at all, but love takes no account of wrong done; it transcends the act of wrong doing.

Joseph

One of the best examples of this type of love is the life of Joseph in Egypt. The favorite son of his father Jacob, Joseph was sold into slavery by his brothers. He was later sent to prison for a crime he didn't commit, only to rise from prison and ascend to the office of prime minister, second in power only to Pharaoh. In the end Joseph forgave his brothers and saved his entire family. Why didn't Joseph become bitter like most others would have in his situation? What gave him the capacity to forgive, even when he had the power to take life? Why is it that there is no account in scripture where Joseph ever complained or felt sorry for himself? I believe it was because he spent time developing in his love walk. You see most of us, particularly those of us in the church, operate on what I call First Level Love. By that I mean the type of love that says: "I love you if you love me. You treat me right, and I'll treat you right. Don't mess with me, and I won't mess with you." This is not the type of love that produces real enduring fruit and results. This love is "tit for tat," immature, and fails to touch the heart of God. Even though Pharaoh was Joseph's captor, Joseph loved him. He loved him so much that he wanted him to receive and know the true and living God. It was this type of love that engaged God's heart and released His power in Joseph's life. Joseph is one of countless examples of biblical men and women who operated within the bounds of God's love, many of whom encountered supernatural occurrences through such love.

Daniel

Like Joseph, Daniel prospered and ruled in a foreign land. In fact he gave meaning to Christ's charge to "Rule thou in the midst of thine enemies." Daniel's influence and power were so great that God delivered him from a den of lions and caused him to prosper through the reign   of six kings. Daniel's love for God and humankind released not only the gift of prophecy and wisdom in his life, but uncommon power and results. Like Joseph, Daniel loved Nebuchadnezzar, Darius, and all of the kings under which he served. This type of love released the anointing of God in his life.

Queen Esther

Another great example of this love is Queen Esther. An orphan girl, Esther ascended through the ranks to become the Queen in a foreign land, and save her nation from extinction. Esther's love for her king, her God, and her people released God's right hand of power and favor as God used both Esther and her cousin, Mordecai in unparalleled fashion. Through Esther's love, salvation and victory came to her people.

King David

Perhaps one of the greatest and purest examples of this kind of love is King David. Born a shepherd boy, and the youngest of his brethren, he loved God, his nation, and his people. Both his love for his sheep, and faithfulness caused him to slay both a lion and a bear. He later faced and defeated the giant Goliath, and became the commander of King Saul's army. David loved King Saul. However, soon jealousy and evil overcame Saul, and he tried to kill David. David was later forced to flee from Saul and even had several opportunities to kill the king. Nevertheless, because of his love for Saul, and his commitment to God, he refused to touch God's anointed king. Because of the love in David's heart, he was eventually anointed king and unifier of Israel. He will be forever remembered as perhaps the greatest king in Israel's history, and "a man after God's own heart."

In more modern times, perhaps one of the best examples of this kind of love is the life of Dr. Martin Luther King, Jr., the great civil rights leader and modern day prophet. If anyone had a right to be bitter, it certainly was him. Consider this bright young preacher who, because of the plight of blacks in America, chose love instead of hate. He chose the path of non-violence, having studied Mohandas K. Gandhi, and how he brought the British Empire to its knees through love. Despite being slandered, arrested, stabbed, harassed, and having his family's home bombed, Dr. King remained committed to love. What was the result? The Montgomery Bus Boycott, the March on Washington, and the passage of the Civil Rights Act. Dr. King's "I Have a Dream Speech" will forever live in the hearts and minds of people throughout the world. Because of Dr. King's decision to walk in love and his sacrifice, he would later win the coveted Nobel Peace Price. To quote scripture, "All run in a race, but only one receives the prize." What prize will walking in love win for you?

What Did Jesus Do?

Consider the qualities and power that Jesus demonstrated on earth. Let's look at all of the qualities of love that the Apostle Paul lists in **I Corinthians 13:4**. Were you to lay all of those qualities over Jesus' life, you would have an exact replica. Let's examine them more closely..

Love	Jesus (Love)
Suffers long	Suffered long - hung on the cross for hours
Kind	Kind - no kinder man ever lived
Envied not	Envied not - envied no man

Love	Jesus (Love)
Vaunted not itself	Vaunted not-didn't have to self -promote
Not puffed up	Not puffed up - made His entry by donkey
Doesn't behave rudely	Didn't behave rudely- loved His enemies
Doesn't seek its own way	Doesn't seek its own way-oriented his life around us
Not easily provoked	Not easily provoked- self control at its best
Thinks no evil	Thought no evil - saw greatness in Peter
Rejoices not in iniquity	Rejoiced not in iniquity - cleansed the temple
Rejoices in truth	Rejoiced in truth - he was the Truth
Bears all things	Bore all things - among them world sin
Believes all things	Believed all things - the best in all people
Endures all things	Endured all things - tempted, but sinless
Never fails	Never failed - He healed them all in Acts 10:38

Wow! Look at the power of love! Jesus was love personified! His life was love displayed at its finest! His power, which was the power of love, caused Him to heal the sick, cast out devils, and even raise the dead. This great power was the ability to create something from nothing, as he turned water into wine at a wedding one day. On one occasion, Jesus fed 5000 people with only two small fish and five loaves of bread from a boy. He even produced money to pay taxes from the mouth of a fish. I like what the Apostle Paul had to say about love at the conclusion of **I Corinthians 13 "And now abideth faith, hope, and love, these three; but the greatest of these is love."** Here

Paul gives us the thing that we should seek or cultivate, if we are to be truly productive in the Kingdom of God: Love.

Love is all-enduring, never wearing out, or becoming obsolete. Love may be the only thing that will never fail us. Again, I uplift **I Corinthians 13: 8** where Paul says, **"But whether there be prophecies, they shall fail; whether there be tongues, they shall cease; whether there be knowledge, it shall vanish away."** The interesting thing here is that Paul tells us not only in what to place our stock, but what will fail us. Paul tells us that love is timeless and unfailing. Love, like Jesus, has withstood the test of time. When everything else has failed, love has been the one constant that has taken a "licking and kept on ticking."

Implementing the Strategy

7 Tactics to Walk In Love on the Battlefield

1. **Pray for your boss.** It is always easy to criticize or complain, but we are commanded in scripture to pray for those in authority. Serve them and help them to become better.

2. **Choose to adopt a good attitude, no matter what.** Our thinking is the only thing that we truly control. Focus only on what you have the power to change, and not on the things you don't. Hebrews 12 says two words that will arrest us in our spirits, "consider Jesus."

3. **Consider the Cross in all things.** Look at everything in comparison to the cross. It is amazing how the cross tends to put life in perspective. The Bible says, "We have not suffered unto bloodshed." One of the great things about the cross is that everything pales in comparison to it.

4. **Develop a heart of gratitude.** Be thankful for everything. Thank God for all that He has done for you. Gratitude is a law of multiplication. Whatever you are grateful for tends to grow.

5. **Study the Word of God.** Study the Gospels, in particular. In studying the life of Christ, we get a very clear perspective on what love looks like. The Beatitudes give great insight into how to walk in love.

6. **Never complain or condemn.** One of the great things about Joseph is that there is no record of him complaining. He chose to become solution-oriented, rather than complaint-oriented. When frustrated about something, look for solutions rather than complain.

7. **Practice walking in love toward someone who is particularly challenging.** Choose someone who is challenging to you and begin to exercise love and self-control toward them. Look for ways to bless them. Listening without judgment or feedback is a great way to walk in love. When tempted to revile, smile. Remember, God takes notice.

As I have traveled the world speaking to all types of people and organizations, one thing is absolutely clear. People, even Christians, have not understood the purpose, power, productivity, and preeminence of love. Many look at it as some goody-goody thing that we learn in nursery rhymes. Others have mistakenly limited it to a romantic feeling that we feel for someone. Love is God's mission. It is who He is. To get a better understanding of love's power, let's examine what **Psalm 97:3** says about God: **"A fire goes before Him and consumes His foes on every side."**

Wow! Look at love's awesome power! Love is a force with which to be reckoned. Since we are made in God's image, we should be imitating God. Fire has the ability to consume and change things. We have that same fire inside of us, possessing that same transformational quality. That fire is called love. Like the lava in a volcano, when we allow that love to rise up in us, it overflows, changing and consuming everything in its path.

Now, you have the weapon. How are you going to use it?

Victory is mine! In the next 7 days, I am going to act on the following in order to Walk In Love:

_____

_____

_____

_____

Chapter 5

Live By Faith

"When you turn to God you discover He has been facing you all the time."
-Zig Ziglar

"The just shall live by faith."
-Habakkuk 2:4

Weapon #4: Live By Faith

Why It Is Powerful

Of all of the great weapons mentioned in this book, the one that binds them all together is faith. The ability to see beyond what is visible is crucial in excelling in life and in the workforce. **Habakkuk 2:4 says, "The just shall live by faith."** Habakkuk meant that faith is not an act, but a lifestyle. The ability to live by faith is so vital because it forces you to trust and depend on God. Faith has the creative power to pull from the unseen realm into the seen. To quote Peter J. Daniels, the great Australian philanthropist, speaker, and entrepreneur, "Faith is the currency of heaven." The important thing to know about faith is this: In order for faith to work it must be spent! **Hebrews 11:6 says, "And without faith it is impossible to please God, because anyone who comes to him must believe that he exists and that he rewards those who earnestly seek him."**

In my travels as a trainer to organizations all over the world, I find a specific constant everywhere: FEAR. Have you listened to people recently? One doesn't have to travel far to realize that fear has gripped the hearts of men and woman today. If you listen, you are likely to hear phrases like: "I'm afraid not." and "What are we going to do now?" Even the music of today tends to be faithless. One of the most popular songs is "I'm All Out of Faith." I don't have anything against the artist or the writer. Obviously, both are very talented. The song has a nice rhythm and beat to it, but I definitely wouldn't recommend belting it out anytime soon if you're looking for faith. This is not coincidental, but by design. Anything that the enemy can do to get you to talk fear instead of faith, he will do. If we are to be truly productive, it is vital that we understand one important point. Satan is after your FAITH! We must understand that everything in the Kingdom of God operates by faith, which works by love.

Strategy for Victory

Action 1: Use Your Mouth as A Divine Weapon of Power

We were created from the mouth of God. Everything started with four words from God's mouth, "Let there be light!" Since we were created in the image of God, we have the same creative power in our mouths. In fact the Word tells us that "life and death are in the power of the tongue." Our words can be used for either good or evil. Yet, we take this great tool – our mouth – for granted.

The first place that anyone can look to determine your faith is your mouth. There is a saying: "People are like sponges, you don't find out what's inside of them until they're squeezed." If you are going to be productive as a Mass Producer, you must speak words of faith at all times and not fear. Fear is how Satan's system works. If he can set you to operate in the fear realm, your faith will not work. The Bible is replete with references of the importance of how we become what we speak.

Action 2: Follow the Law of Divine Drafting

Have you ever seen cyclists compete in the Tour de France? One of the most celebrated cyclists from that race is seven-time Tour de France champion, Lance Armstrong. After being diagnosed with cancer, he bounces back and wins yet another championship against all odds! What a great example of achieving the impossible. These tremendously well conditioned athletes travel up mountains and endure all types of arduous gradation changes. When you consider the difficulty of the race, it doesn't seem possible for the human body to endure such demands. Yet, cyclists have a special method called drafting. The way the process works is that the cyclists form a line behind the lead cyclist. When they are all aligned properly, there is a wind current that literally pulls them through. This process allows the cyclists to conserve their energy, and not rely solely on their own strength. Savvy champion cyclists know how to use this process to their benefit to enable them to perform at unbelievable levels.

In like manner, there is a restful power in God in which we can enter when performing. I call it "The Law of Divine Drafting." The "Law of Divine Drafting" states that when we align our wills, hearts, spirits, and efforts with God's will, we will make supernatural progress at an astounding pace. We are not operating in our strength alone, but in God's as well. We are restored much faster and tend to be less fatigued. There is a divine ease, grace, peace, and power over our performance. My pastor calls it "Sweatless Victory."

Have you ever noticed a certain grace and power while operating in your gift or on your job? Perhaps you are working on a particular project at work. Suddenly and out of nowhere, this second wind seems to kick in. That is "The Law of Divine Drafting" at work. How many of you have ever been restored in some area of your life at a supernaturally accelerated rate? This is what we have to look forward to as children of God. We don't have to be in gloom, doom, and despair; there is a rest for the people of God to enter into, but we must access it by faith. It is in exercising our faith by our expectations, words, and actions, that we engage this wonderful law to assist us.

Action 3: Give Faith a Voice...Yours!

One of the things that I love about Jesus is His continual emphasis on the power of our words. He frequently used the word "you." He is constantly reminding us of how great we are and the authority of our words. He wanted you to understand a foundational truth: Faith has a voice...yours! One of the things that we must understand about faith is that we must speak it.

The Bible says that a man or a woman is a "speaking spirit." That means that your words have weight, and you must use them. Why do you suppose Joshua says, **"Do not let this Book depart from**

before your mouth." (Joshua 1:8) The minute you open your mouth, it doesn't take long to discover who you are. One morning as I was waiting for an elevator, I asked a man waiting also, how he was doing. He replied, "Pretty good, I guess. I fear winter will come early this year." He looked worried and miserable. I smiled and responded, "Hopefully it will come later than planned." His expression and words said it all. You could tell that he was paralyzed by fear.   In like manner, faith speaks. Now let me pause here and say that I can certainly understand and empathize with the gentleman. There is no way for us to know what someone has faced in their lifetime. The point I would like to make here, is that God gives us faith as a better alternative to fear.

One of the greatest examples of faith speaking can be seen in the life of David. As a teenage boy, his father Jesse sent him to the battlefront with wine and cheese for his brothers. At that time the Philistines were running roughshod over the army of Israel, led by King Saul. The Philistine soldiers laughed as their champion Goliath taunted Israel with his insults. In brash audacity, he called for King Saul to send him a man to fight in single combat. This battle would determine the outcome of the war. Goliath, a menacing giant standing nearly ten feet tall, left the Israelites shaking in their boots. As the giant brandished his heavy spear and ridiculed the courage of Israel, the soldiers' hearts failed them out of fear.

As David, little more than a child half Goliath's size, approached the battle line, he heard the giant shout insults about Jehovah. David loved God with a pure heart. Lying under the stars at night, he would often bask in God's presence, as he later recorded the Psalms. His fellowship was unbroken by the cares of this world. Everywhere in nature he looked, David saw the handiwork of God – in the hills, in the trees, in the blue skies, and even in God's protective hand as he killed dangerous lions and bears. He was tried and tested. Though only a boy in age, the Bible declares that he was a MAN after God's own heart. This Philistine had no idea what he had gotten himself into.

Upon arriving to meet his brothers, David inquired, "Who is this uncircumcised Philistine that he should defy the living God?" What audacity! It sounds to me like he knew who his God was! Initially, the enemy attempted to slow him down through his older brother, Eliab. Eliab asked David, "Why did you come down here? And with whom have ye left those few sheep in the wilderness?" David asked a very important question, "Is there not a cause?" Listen to his faith!

Everything about him was an indication of his confidence in his God.

He eventually approached King Saul and asked, "What shall be done for the man that kills that Philistine?" Upon being told that he would receive the king's daughter's hand in marriage, David agreed to fight the Giant. Saul even offered his armor and sword to David. However, David chose his own familiar weaponry, a slingshot.

David went down to meet the giant, as the battle was about to commence. As David approached, fear attempted to talk to David through the giant's mouth. In I Samuel 17:43 Goliath bellowed, "Am I a dog that thou cometh to me with staves? Come unto me, and I will give thy flesh unto the fowls of the air, and to the beasts of the field." Instead of fear, David responded with the fury of faith, saying, "Thou cometh to me with a sword, and with a spear, and with a shield: but I come to thee in the name of the LORD of hosts, the God of the armies of Israel, whom thou hast defied. This day will the LORD deliver thee into mine hand; and I will give the carcasses of the host of the Philistines this day unto the fowls of the air, and to the wild beast of the earth; that all the earth may know that there is a God in Israel."

Wow! Listen to faith speak! Such faith and confidence shows why David was a man after God's own heart. Victory after those words was imminent, as David knocked the giant to the ground with one shot, and proceeded to decapitate the giant with his own sword. All of the Philistines fled in terror, as the triumphant shepherd lifted the giant's head before the armies of God.

Although this is a great story, the main point that I'd like to emphasize is this: David's actions only followed his faith-filled words! What if David had spoken fear? What if he allowed the fear to talk to him with no rebuttal? I would submit to you that we would have a very different story. Nevertheless, today we celebrate this victory. We look back with inspiration, as we remember that day that all of Israel was restored by the faith of a young lad that spoke faith. Likewise, when we speak faith, we have the power to direct our outcomes. Below are seven tactics to live by the faith of David.

Implementing the Strategy

7 Tactics to Live By Faith on the Battlefield

1. Speak Faith. Watch the words that come out of your mouth. Ensure that they line up with God's word. Your employer is looking for "Good News," whether they know it or not. Be the possibility person in your company. Don't bring back an evil report.

2. Prove God. Activate your faith. Give God something to work with. Don't always play it too safe.

3. Listen to the Word. Have the Word of God playing as often as you can within certain parameters. Romans 10:17 says, "So then faith cometh by hearing, and hearing by the word of God."

4. Study the Word. Read your Bible often. Get it in your heart. It will bless you tremendously and increase your faith.

5. Pray. One of the greatest ways to increase your faith is spending time with God in prayer. You cannot spend intimate time with God and remain the same. When you spend time with God, you take on God's thoughts, and learn God's ways.

6. Attend Teachings at Church. Sitting under great teaching is a great way to increase your faith. If necessary, make it a point to utilize technology properly to hear the lessons.

7. Fellowship with Others in Faith. Remove yourself from negative people who drain your faith and make it a point to spend more time with other Christians who will charge your faith.

Faith allows us to partner with God to manifest the good that God has for us and to be the mass producers He wants us to be.

Now, you have the weapon. How are you going to use it?

Victory is mine! In the next 7 days, I am going to act on the following in order to Live By Faith:

_____

_____

_____

Chapter 6

Inspire Yourself

"I will persist, I will prepare, and my opportunity will come!"
-Abraham Lincoln

"But David encouraged himself in the Lord His God."
Ist Samuel 30:6

Weapon #5: Inspire Yourself

Why It Is Powerful

The ability to inspire ourselves is one of the most crucial abilities we must possess as Mass Producers. Unfortunately, the ability to inspire one's self is a tremendous problem in our nation today because of the limited understanding of inspiration and how to acquire it. Regrettably, many believe inspiration should come solely from an external source, like great historical figures, charismatic leaders, music, friends or family, or even a supervisor or manager. Now let me be the first say that I believe that any good manager or supervisor should certainly inspire their employees. But what happens when they don't? Have you ever had the experience of working with a boss or manager who was unreliable – who did not do what they said they would when they said they would do it? I imagine probably almost every day. Here is what I have discovered: We can inspire ourselves. Those who are waiting for their bosses to inspire them will be waiting for a long time. The employer and the employee must work together in unison for inspiration to be cultivated.

The word "inspire" comes from the Latin root "inspirari," which means "to breathe life into." I love this word because it is what God did to Adam when He created him. Now it is very important here that I make a distinction between inspiration and motivation. As a trainer for almost a decade, one of the biggest requests I receive from organizations is: "We want to motivate our people!" While motivation is a good thing, and a vital part of inspiration, I find that it tends to be two things: short lived and seasonal. For example, have you ever known someone to be motivated to lose weight? How long did it last typically? Maybe not very long. The word "motivation" is comprised of two words, "motive" and "action." In other words, as long as it is something that I want, then I'll combine it with action. Let me reiterate here that I believe that motivation is a great thing. There is nothing wrong with it. There are many changes in our lives that will only happen as a result of motivation – from starting a diet to ending a destructive addiction.

However, the personal tendency of motivation can omit the larger blessing that God desires for us as His people. God is always concerned about blessing more than just us individually. His concern is always the entire blessing of humankind. He desires to bless you so that you can be a blessing to others. Inspiration, on the other hand, comes from God; it encompasses more than just you. You see, when God is involved, it is always better, and includes more people. When people are inspired, truly inspired, they do greater things that are longer lasting, and are of higher quality. In order to determine the difference between inspiration and motivation, I asked myself a very important question. This question forever solidified the answer for me. The question was this: "What is the result when people are truly inspired?" If you are managing people, perhaps this will be a question that will help you develop your employees. Here are some of the answers I came up with:

Under the inspiration of God, a teenage boy named David slew a giant named Goliath, who was nearly ten feet tall, with only a slingshot. Under that same inspiration, David previously killed a lion and a bear.

Inspiration caused an average sized man named Samson to slay 1000 Philistines with only the jawbone of an ass. (Talk about inadequate resources!) It was reported that this one man terrorized the nation of Philistia.

Under the inspiration of God, two million Jews, led by a stuttering prophet named Moses, walked across the Red Sea on dry land. After previously being under Egyptian captivity, they left with that nation's wealth in tow. This same inspiration caused this same prophet to break the back of Egypt with only a stick. God used this same stick to part the sea.

Under the inspiration of God, America, led by General George Washington, gained her independence from England. Through frostbite, death, and disease, they managed to defeat a superior British army with only volunteer militia.

Inspiration propelled over one million African Americans and other Americans to assemble in Washington, DC. They traveled to take a stand for civil rights and justice for all Americans. They witnessed history when Dr. Martin Luther King, Jr. delivered the famous "I Have A Dream" speech. This compelling speech, delivered by this Nobel Prize winner is considered by many as perhaps the greatest speech in American history. On this day, Black America truly became free.

Under the inspiration of God, Harriet Tubman, a woman called "Moses," led over three hundred enslaved Africans to freedom in the North. Though she had Narcolepsy, the "Sleeping Disease," she was never captured, and the Underground Railroad served as a liberating route from captivity.

Under the inspiration of God, a 34-year-old literature professor turned colonel named Joshua Chamberlain dealt a lethal blow to the Confederate army. With no ammunition left, and only eighty men, he led the charge at the Battle of "Little Round Top," capturing over four hundred enemy soldiers. Armed with only bayonets, courage, and inspiration, he led our nation to victory. This battle at Gettysburg, was said to be the pivotal battle in deciding the Civil War.

Under the inspiration of God, President Abraham Lincoln signed the Emancipation Proclamation, ending the institution of slavery in America, freeing the enslaved, and paving the way for America to achieve greatness as a nation.

Hopefully, by now you are beginning to get the picture. When people are inspired, it is an amazing thing to behold. They perform far above what may be considered to be a normal ability. They disarm difficulties, and achieve the impossible. King David said it best in **II Samuel 22:30 "For by my God I have run through a troop, and by my God, I have leapt over a wall."** When people are inspired, a divine providence overshadows them, robbing even death of its power until the successful fulfillment of their destinies. They do things that are eternal and long-lasting, as opposed to things that are temporal and bound by time. When men and women are inspired, they think the unthinkable, reach the unreachable, and achieve the impossible.

Strategy for Victory

Action 1: Recognize the Transformational Power of Inspiration

One of the great attributes of true inspiration is courage. Those who are truly inspired, soon learn that the safest place on earth is in the will of God. How different many organizations would be if they fully understood the importance of inspiration. When people are inspired, neither their thinking nor their actions are average. They are not relegated to this finite world in which we live. They are tuned into God's channel. They look and act like who they were created to be, sons and daughters of God. Perhaps that is why the Apostle Paul, in writing to the Corinthians, asked a powerful question in amazement. In **I Corinthians 3:3** he asks, **"Are you not acting like mere humans?"** Why was he so shocked? Perhaps it was because He knew the transformational power and effect of inspiration on humankind. In **Genesis 2:7** it records: **"Then the LORD God formed a man from the dust of the ground and breathed into his nostrils the breath of life, and the man became a living being."** When God created humankind, he breathed the very life of God into us. The thing that He breathed into us was called "Zoe Life," the part of God that makes Him who He is. One translation calls it, "The wind and breath of Jehovah."

Action 2: Realize the Power of Words

Our mouths have the same transformational power. **Proverbs 18:21** says, **"The tongue has the power of life and death, and those who love it will eat its fruit."** I have a very important question for you: What are your words producing? Do they produce life, inspiring and encouraging others to greatness? Or do they produce death and doubt, enacting failure and mediocrity? We must remember that God created everything that we see by speaking. Since we are made in His image and likeness, we have the same power in our mouths.

It is vitally important that we handle this very special power with care. How many young lives have been derailed because of words of death being spoken over them? How many years have been wasted due to careless conversations? We must speak words of life over ourselves and others. Remember, it was through the mouth of God that life was breathed into us. By the same token, we, by our words, have the ability to speak life to other people. The real challenge that I find with most of us is not in speaking life to others, but to ourselves. In fact, the ability to encourage others comes out of our ability to encourage ourselves. If we are to be victorious, it is vital that we only speak words of life to ourselves, instead of words of death.

Have you ever called yourself stupid? Whenever we do that, we are programming ourselves for failure, because our subconscious mind simply obeys what we tell it. Your subconscious mind is very indiscriminating. It simply obeys the instruction that you give it. Have you ever done something stupid after calling yourself stupid? Why did that happen? Because you gave it an instruction of "stupid," and it gave you back, "stupid."

Action 3: Remember the Goodness of God

One of the greatest examples of inspiring oneself is found in I Samuel 30. As the scene unfolds, David and his men come back from fighting a battle at Ziklag. Upon arriving, they discover that the Amalekites had invaded their camp. Not only have they invaded their camp, but they have kidnapped their wives and children, burning their camp to the ground. Nothing is left standing, as the Amalekites have made off with the spoil. All of the men weep with anguish, as they weep until there is no strength left in them. The men then turn their frustrations on David, and even speak of stoning him. He is perplexed and distressed. Can you imagine the stress and anguish that David experienced? It is difficult to even comprehend the bewilderment, pain, anger, and chaos of the camp at that time.

In I Samuel 30:6 it reads: **"David was greatly distressed because the men were talking of stoning him; each one was bitter in spirit because of his sons and daughters. But David found strength in the LORD his God."** David used the great reserve of memorials and experiences he had with God to inspire himself. He had spent so much time in God's presence and in fellowship with God that he knew God intimately. He talked with God, and God talked with him. One of the best ways that God communicated with David was showing His power on David's behalf. David had a spectacular memorial and arsenal of adventures with God that he could draw on, meditate on, and rely on for encouragement. Notice, the passage does not record that David waited on God to inspire Him. David took the initiative to engage God by using his faith. It was only after doing so, that God moved on his behalf.

How many people do you know who are sitting around waiting for God to inspire them? Many people think that God is supposed to do all of the work. Not so. God has given us the authority to use what we have. Isn't it interesting that another name for the Holy Spirit is "Helper?" Why didn't God call him the "doer?" I believe because humankind has a role to play in the process. The first thing that David had to do was remember the goodness of God. Our first inclination, when seemingly impending doom is upon us, is to ask, "God, why did you let this to happen to me?" In doing so, we don't even realize that we are blaming God, and allowing fear to control us.

We human beings have a very short memory. We tend to quickly forget the blessings that we just received from God. Why do you suppose God reiterates the word "remember" over and over? Perhaps it is because He knew the impulsive, fickle, and flaky nature, apart from Him. He knew that if we did not discipline ourselves in order to consciously and deliberately remember and meditate on His goodness, we would forget. The word "remember" is mentioned 148 times in the King James Version, and 167 times in the New International Version of the Bible. What was the result of David encouraging himself in the Lord? The total recovery of all he lost, including all of the spoil of the Amalekites.

I Samuel 30 gives this account:

[7] Then David said to Abiathar the priest, the son of Ahimelek, "Bring me the ephod." Abiathar brought it to him, [8] and David inquired of the LORD, "Shall I pursue this raiding party? Will I overtake them?"

"Pursue them," he answered. "You will certainly overtake them and succeed in the rescue."

[9] David and the six hundred men with him came to the Besor Valley, where some stayed behind. [10] Two hundred of them were too exhausted to cross the valley, but David and the other four hundred continued the pursuit.

11 **They found an Egyptian in a field and brought him to David. They gave him water to drink and food to eat— 12 part of a cake of pressed figs and two cakes of raisins. He ate and was revived, for he had not eaten any food or drunk any water for three days and three nights.**

13 David asked him, "Who do you belong to? Where do you come from?"

He said, "I am an Egyptian, the slave of an Amalekite. My master abandoned me when I became ill three days ago. 14 We raided the Negev of the Kerethites, some territory belonging to Judah and the Negev of Caleb. And we burned Ziklag."

15 David asked him, "Can you lead me down to this raiding party?"

He answered, "Swear to me before God that you will not kill me or hand me over to my master, and I will take you down to them."

16 He led David down, and there they were, scattered over the countryside, eating, drinking and reveling because of the great amount of plunder they had taken from the land of the Philistines and from Judah. 17 David fought them from dusk until the evening of the next day, and none of them got away, except four hundred young men who rode off on camels and fled. 18 David recovered everything the Amalekites had taken, including his two wives. 19 Nothing was missing: young or old, boy or girl, plunder or anything else they had taken. David brought everything back. 20 He took all the flocks and herds, and his men drove them ahead of the other livestock, saying, "This is David's plunder."

Because David was able to inspire himself, he was able to save his entire following. He not only recovered all, but gained the spoil of both the Amalekites and the Philistines, as well. God delivered on everything that he promised David, and, as is His nature, gave him much more than He promised. The thing that I would like to draw your attention to here is that David's will, not his emotions, were responsible for the breakthrough. He did not panic or succumb to the pressure, but took authority over his emotions. Even though he felt like caving in, he took action.

Implementing the Strategy

7 (Plus 4 Bonus) Tactics to Inspire Yourself on the Battlefield

Your Inspirational Arsenal

In order for us to stay inspired, it is important for us to put together an inspirational arsenal. What inspires you? Since inspiration is our responsibility, I recommend that you engage this process by drawing from several sources of inspiration. Usually, I list seven tactics or keys to aid you on the battlefield. Here, I am providing four bonus ways to inspire yourself.

1. **Music** – To quote my good friend and creator of the wonderful *Bible Experience*, Lou "Buster" Brown, "Music is a place." Isn't it amazing how the right music can inspire you, evoking in you feelings of joy, resolve, confidence, and love? Find the music that inspires you and keep it around you. I really enjoy both contemporary gospel music, as well as the traditional hymns of the church. It doesn't necessarily have to be limited to gospel, but it should have an upbeat, inspirational message. Movie themes are particularly powerful. How many of you remember the movie "Rocky." It's amazing how just listening to a few bars from the theme song, "Gonna Fly Now," by Bill Conti can immediately inspire us all to start working out.

2. **Famous Quotes** – One of the powerful things that we can include in our arsenal are famous quotes. Quotes have an interesting way of arresting us in our spirits when we are in a complaining mood. They can also inspire us to stand tall in times of indecision. Hearing a quote from the great Earl Nightingale inspired me to become a speaker. Who inspires you? They may no longer be alive, but their influence can live long after they are gone.

3. **Inspirational Achievement Scrapbook** – Put together a scrapbook of the things that you have accomplished so that you can go back and reflect on those experiences. Many times in life, when referring to the past, there is a tendency dwell on our failures, and the things that we have done wrong. This is a strategy that Satan uses to stifle our productivity. The apostle Paul had a different formula. In the book of Philippians, he exhorts us to meditate on things which are good, just, pure, lovely, and of good report. Celebrate you! Remember, if you

don't do it on purpose, chances are good to excellent that you will forget. Keep an active visual of your successful you.

4. **Movies** – Perhaps of one of the biggest, and most powerful of all inspirational sources is movies. Movies do a great job of capturing the heart, capturing the moments, and freezing them in time. Be sure to have some of the most inspiring DVDs and videos in your arsenal, so that you can go back and watch them at times when you need to be lifted up. You will be amazed at what they do for your spirit.

5. **Biographies** – Biographies are some of the greatest contributors to your inspirational arsenal. Biographies are tremendously powerful, in that they are real life accounts of great people who experienced many of the challenges that we face. I learned this from hearing Australian philanthropist Peter J. Daniels speak. He said that one of the things that changed his life was reading 2000 biographies. Biographies are great, in that they chronicle the lives of people who overcame insurmountable odds. When we read about the struggles that great people overcame, we identify with it, and it resonates with us. When we get their story in our spirit, we realize two very important things: 1) If they can do it, so can I. 2) I am not the only one encountering challenges in life. Biographies have been largely responsible for making some of the great even greater.

6. **The Bible** – I don't know of any more inspirational document to have in your arsenal than the Bible. It is the world's only timeless living document. I call it living because it is inexhaustible. By that I mean it is the only book ever written whereby one can read it for years and still find a revelation. Hebrews 4:12 says, "For the word of God is alive and active. Sharper than any double-edged sword, it penetrates even to dividing soul and spirit, joints and marrow; it judges the thoughts and attitudes of the heart." It is very important that we understand that the Bible is not a novel, but a manual for life instruction. It contains everything from proper parenting to victorious marriages to sound money management. The Bible also is a snapshot of you. It is a reminder of who you are and where you came from. To quote Kenneth Copeland, "The Bible is sixty-six volume victory statement." It reminds you who you are because, by nature, we are quick to forget if we do not read God's Word. Nobody knows you like the one who made you. The Bible is His love letter to you.

7. **Inspiring People** – Who inspires you? Optimists are the saviors of the world. Who are the people in your life who encouraged you to do something when you thought you couldn't? Who is the person who pushed you to face that bully or conquer fear when you thought you couldn't? I have found that some of the greatest sources of inspiration are people who sincerely care about you and your success. Now I'd like to stop here and make an important distinction. I am not talking about being dependent on people or expecting them to do your part for you. I am also not talking about being beholding to people or being in bondage to them by manipulation. I am speaking of those special people - genuine relationships that God has placed in your life to be a blessing to you. Many times these special people see things in us that we do not see in ourselves. Thank God for them.

8. **Prayer** – Arguably the most vital of all weapons in your inspirational arsenal is the weapon of prayer. Luke 18:1 says we "ought always to pray and not to faint." The Amplified Bible says it this way: "Also Jesus told them a parable to the effect that they ought always to pray, not to turn coward, faint, lose heart, and give up." In reading this scripture, it is vitally important that we understand that prayer must be a lifestyle. How many times have you been in a situation that seemed hopeless, only to pray and see God's power? Perhaps the breakthrough came through a miraculous change of events or change of fortune. Maybe the breakthrough came through God changing your heart regarding the matter. Or maybe the circumstances didn't change, but your perspective did. Where there was fear, perhaps God gave you courage and an amazing peace.

    The point that I'd like to make here is that when you communicate with God, great things happen. When the disciples prayed for boldness, they were inspired to achieve miraculous results. Let's examine what happened after this prayer. In Acts 17:6 the Romans described the disciples in the following way: "These men who have caused trouble all over the world have now come here..." When we pray, we can turn our world upside down as well.

9. **Confession of the Word of God** – Jesus said in John 6:63: "My words, they are spirit and they are life." We have previously said that life and death are in the power of

the tongue. Begin to confess God's word over your life daily. Write down scriptures that correspond with what you desire to see changed in your life. Speak them to yourself, and you will be amazed at how they transform you. Your confidence will soar, and your faith will begin to kick in. When you say what God says about you, you are literally pre-programming yourself for success and victory. Many of us have the tendency to say negative things to ourselves such as "That was stupid." or "You idiot!"

This is crucial for two reasons. 1) When we speak to ourselves in negative self talk, we speak to ourselves twice as fast as when we talk to ourselves positively. 2) We are setting ourselves up for failure in countering the positive words that we have spoken. When you begin to speak to yourself in faith and expectation, there is conversion that takes place in your heart. You become the giant God intended you to be. That "grasshopper mentality" cannot withstand the constant onslaught of God's word. It is very important that we not underestimate the power of God's word in our mouths. The word of God is not hindered or limited by our finite logical reasoning that the world tends to operate in. It is a creative force that will change and rearrange situations, causing them to bow in homage to it, and to bend around it. The only limitations to it are the ones that you place around it. The great thing about repetition is this: whatever we hear long enough, we tend to believe. Begin today to speak victory over yourself, and see your self image soar.

10. **Laugh** – Nehemiah 8:10 says, "The joy of the LORD is our strength." God wants you to laugh. Cultivate joy in your life. Create a joyful disposition, and laugh often. It has been said that the reasons angels can fly is because they take themselves so lightly. Have you ever noticed how unproductive and stale you become when you take yourself too seriously? God did not intend for you to walk around with pursed lips, tight jaws, and a face that looks like a catcher's mitt. He wants you to have a joyful, loving, and fun disposition. As a Christian, you have so much for which to be grateful. I also recommend that you document and keep a record of particular funny moments in your life. Refer to them often to keep yourself inspired. Smile. Let people have to interrupt your personal celebration when they meet you. Jesus laughed often. Learn to laugh at yourself.

Tim Hansel, author of You Gotta Keep Dancin' says, "He [or she] that has learned to laugh at oneself shall never cease to be amused." Make sure to have some friends that make you laugh.

Have you ever noticed how resilient you are when you are joyful? Things tend to simply bounce off of you. That is because joy is the elasticity in your rubber band. Have you ever ridden the bumper cars at the fair or amusement park? If you have, then you have noticed a rubber bumper around the base. That bumper is designed to absorb the shock causing the cars to bounce off of the other cars with no damage. That is precisely the effect God intended joy to have in your life.

It is a divine insulator from the damage inflicted by the enemy. When joy is heightened, your creativity flows freely and your confidence, valor, and risk-taking nature are released. Perhaps that is why it says in the book of Proverbs, "A merry heart does good like a medicine." Be sure to take your daily dose of laughter and stay inspired.

11. **Avoiding the News in the Morning.** One of the greatest methods for maintaining our inspiration is avoiding the news upon waking in the morning. Although the news can be a tremendous source of information, it can be a great destroyer of your inspiration. Have you ever found yourself waking up to the news first thing in the morning? I know many of us have been doing it for years because we have been programmed to do so. Perhaps you do it because you want to know what the weather will be like. Maybe you are a sports fan, and you want to know whether your team won last night. The problem with this type of news is that it's usually bad news. The breaking story of the hour can usually be anything from somebody dying to some national disaster. Why is this? Unfortunately bad news is good press and it fuels sales. Satan has ingeniously designed it so that he can bombard your spirit with negativity before even start your day. If he can get you fatigued in your mind, you'll begin your day in fear and dread going to work, and be defeated mentally before you start.

This is why our first communication upon awaking should be with God. The book of Daniel talks about how Satan desires to wear out the saints of the most high. It is vital that upon waking and praying we read our Bible. When we do so, we garrison our minds from the onslaught of the devil and create the mindset of Christ. Studies show that the first thirty minutes of the day are of vital importance. The first thirty minutes of the day have been called by some as the thirty magic moments. Why is this so important? Because whatever you tend to put in your mind the first thirty minutes of the day tends to set the tempo of the day. Whenever you start your day with tragedy, you tend to have a tragic day. Brian Tracy, in his wonderful audio program, "The Psychology of Achievement," speaks of this great strategy. He says that we should start each day putting rich mental protein into our minds by reading something inspirational and uplifting.

It is imperative that we value the importance of inspiration in determining our outcomes. We must always remember that apart from God we can do nothing. According to **Philippians 4:13** **"We can do all things through Him."** Since inspiration comes from God, it is God we must engage. We must honor Him, revere Him, and seek His direction in all of our affairs. Hopefully, you will develop your own inspirational arsenal if needed. Am I suggesting that you have to use any, some, or all of these. Absolutely not. I am not claiming to corner the market on knowing what does or does not inspire people. What I am saying is that I have found that it is far better to have more than you need than to need and not have enough. Whatever you must do to inspire yourself ethically, I recommend that you do it. I do not, however, recommend that you do nothing.

Now, you have the weapon. How are you going to use it?

Victory is mine! In the next 7 days, I will act on the following in order to Inspire Myself:

_____

_____

_____

_____

Chapter 7

Praise God!

*"If you're sincere, praise is effective.
If you're insincere, it's manipulative."*

-Zig Ziglar

*"Yet you are enthroned as the Holy One;
you are the one Israel praises."*

-Psalm 22:3

Weapon #6: Praise God!

Why It Is Powerful

Praise God! How many times in your life have you made that statement? Attend most any church service and you will likely hear theses words. Yet, how very few people truly understand their power. The weapon of praise is potent. Praise is powerful because it paralyzes Satan and sends him into derision and confusion. Praise rattles Satan's cage, and scrambles his radar! The word praise comes from the Latin word, "pretium," which means "price." It literally means to "place a great price on." When you praise God, you are placing a high price on God by thanking God for what He has done in your life.

What makes praise so potent against the enemy?

Praise is born out of gratitude, which is the opposite of pride. Gratitude is a law of multiplication. When you are grateful for things in your life, they tend to grow. That's why sometimes a simple, "Thank you, Lord" is the most powerful prayer. Satan, on the other hand, operates by pride. It was the same pride that made him say, "I will exalt my throne above the most high, and I will be like God."

Praise reminds Satan of the job that he lost. Satan had the best job in the universe. He was the holy beautiful Lucifer, the chief worship leader. All he did day and night was to praise and worship God. He was the head worshipper in heaven. How can anyone be stupid enough to lose a job like that and get kicked out of heaven? When he got kicked out, you and I got his job! When you praise God, you make Satan replay that nightmarish rerun of his failure, over and over again.

Praise detours your mind from your insufficiency, and reroutes your focus to God's limitless sufficiency and endless supply. Praise turns your mentality from one of scarcity and lack to one of overflowing abundance, supply, and power.

When we praise God, we bring His presence into our life and circumstances in a powerful way. **Psalm 22:3** says, **"Yet you are enthroned as the Holy One; you are the one Israel praises."** God inhabits the praises of God's people. When we praise God, He takes a seat at the table of our lives and dwells with us. That's why praise and worship music is so powerful because you are literally singing your victory ahead of time. You are doing what you were created to do, which is to worship God and give Him glory.

The beautiful thing about praise and worship music is there is something for everyone. Maybe your favorite is "Again, I Say Rejoice," by Israel and New Breed, or Chris Tomlin's, "How Great Is Our God." Perhaps it is Marvin Sapp's, "Never Would Have Made It," or Michael W. Smith's "Heart of Worship." Whether your taste is contemporary gospel, or more traditional, God has something for everyone's style and taste. The important point I'd like to emphasize is that when you praise God, you are inviting Him to take a seat at the table of your heart.

Strategy for Victory

If we are to truly do warfare in the spirit realm, we must be willing to open our mouths and thank God for His marvelous work in our lives. Now, in our natural mind, this does not make good sense as a military strategy. However, the Bible is vividly clear about a very important point. Some of the most spectacular battles in biblical history have been won as a direct result of praise.

One such battle was King Jehoshaphat in II Chronicles 20. As the scene unfolds, King Jehoshaphat is facing his toughest test of leadership to date. The surrounding nations of Ammon, Moab, and Mount Seir, come to attack Judah. The King's servant warned that a great multitude was coming against him. King Jehoshaphat does not know what to do, but he decides to proclaim a fast throughout Judah. As he stands before the assembly, he praises and worships God by opening his mouth and reminding God verbally of who God is and what God has done. He begins to reference God's track record of victory! **II Chronicles 20:4-12** records it this way:

⁴ The people of Judah came together to seek help from the LORD; indeed, they came from every town in Judah to seek him.

⁵ Then Jehoshaphat stood up in the assembly of Judah and Jerusalem at the temple of the LORD in the front of the new courtyard ⁶ and said:

"LORD, the God of our ancestors, are you not the God who is in heaven? You rule over all the kingdoms of the nations. Power and might are in your hand, and no one can withstand you. ⁷ Our God, did you not drive out the inhabitants of this land before your people Israel and give it forever to the descendants of Abraham your friend? ⁸ They have lived in it and have built in it a sanctuary for your Name, saying, ⁹ 'If calamity comes upon us, whether the sword of judgment, or plague or famine, we will stand in your presence before this temple that bears your Name and will cry out to you in our distress, and you will hear us and save us.'

¹⁰ "But now here are men from Ammon, Moab and Mount Seir, whose territory you would not allow Israel to invade when they came from Egypt; so they turned away from them and did not destroy them. ¹¹ See how they are repaying us by coming to

**drive us out of the possession you gave us as an inheritance. ¹²
Our God, will you not judge them? For we have no power to face
this vast army that is attacking us. We do not know what to do,
but our eyes are on you."**

Listen to Jehoshaphat's praise and worship. He begins with this
rhetorical question: "LORD, the God of our ancestors, are you not the
God who is in heaven?" Here, Jehoshaphat asks a question to which
he obviously knows the answer. He is praising God by telling Him
how great He is. This is the essence of true praise and worship. Praise
is thanking God for what He has done, but worship is thanking God for
who He is.

He reminds both God and himself of the past victories that
they have experienced together as a result of God's hand. When
Jehoshaphat begins to do this, two interesting dynamics begin to
happen simultaneously. God gets turned on, and Jehoshaphat begins
to be encouraged. Have you ever noticed how praising God takes
your mind off of your circumstances and directs it to God where
it belongs? Perhaps that is why the Word tells us to cast all of our
care on God for God cares for us. He even begins to remind God
how these enemies are attacking God's honor and glory. What I love
best about this prayer is how real and honest Jehoshaphat is with
God. Never does he claim to have all of the answers. His confidence
rests not in his own ability, but in his God's. **"Our God, will you not
judge them? For we have no power to face this vast army that is
attacking us. We do not know what to do, but our eyes are on you."
(II Chronicles 20:12)**

What honesty and purity of heart! What total confidence and
dependence on God's ability! He is literally saying, "God, we have
absolutely no clue what to do in this situation, but we know that you
do, and our eyes are on you God!" It is this prayer that moves the
heart of God. Immediately following his prayer, the Spirit of the Lord
shows up, and comes on a man named Jahaziel. "Then the Spirit of
the LORD came on Jahaziel son of Zechariah, the son of Benaiah, the
son of Jeiel, the son of Mattaniah, a Levite and descendant of Asaph,
as he stood in the assembly." **(II Chronicles 20:14)**

**¹⁵ He said: "Listen, King Jehoshaphat and all who live in Judah
and Jerusalem! This is what the LORD says to you: 'Do not be
afraid or discouraged because of this vast army. For the battle
is not yours, but God's. ¹⁶ Tomorrow march down against them.
They will be climbing up by the Pass of Ziz, and you will find**

them at the end of the gorge in the Desert of Jeruel. ¹⁷ You will not have to fight this battle. Take up your positions; stand firm and see the deliverance the LORD will give you, Judah and Jerusalem. Do not be afraid; do not be discouraged. Go out to face them tomorrow, and the LORD will be with you.'"

¹⁸ Jehoshaphat bowed down with his face to the ground, and all the people of Judah and Jerusalem fell down in worship before the LORD. ¹⁹ Then some Levites from the Kohathites and Korahites stood up and praised the LORD, the God of Israel, with a very loud voice.

²⁰ Early in the morning they left for the Desert of Tekoa. As they set out, Jehoshaphat stood and said, "Listen to me, Judah and people of Jerusalem! Have faith in the LORD your God and you will be upheld; have faith in his prophets and you will be successful." ²¹ After consulting the people, Jehoshaphat appointed men to sing to the LORD and to praise him for the splendor of his holiness as they went out at the head of the army, saying:

"Give thanks to the LORD, for his love endures forever."
II Chronicles 20: 15-21

Let's get the picture. The Lord tells Jehoshaphat to not be afraid or discouraged due to the great army because this fight belongs to the Lord. He goes on further to assure Jehoshaphat that he will not even have to fight, but that he should stand firm and see God's hand of deliverance over his enemies. Imagine God saying to you, there will be no need to fight, just pull up a good seat, grab some popcorn, and watch me destroy your enemies. Glory to God!

Now I would like to pause here for a moment and take a station break at a pivotal point in this story, the moment of decision. It is here, in the midst of the euphoria, that battles are either won or lost. It is here that Jehoshaphat passes the leadership test by making the right decision. You see Jehoshaphat had a choice to make. He came to a point that we all must come to in our lives: To believe or not to believe? He could have relied on his logical, analytical mind and decided not to listen to the prophet of God. I mean, after all, he was the king. He could have said, "You want me to do what?" You want me to send my praise team out front with no weapons? He could have taken counsel from the popular voices of the day to make sure he was being "politically" correct, but morally bankrupt. He could have decided that the office of king was superior to that of a prophet, and refused to listen to him, as we see so often today. He could have allowed pride and competition to separate those two great offices that God designed to walk shoulder to shoulder together in power. Instead, as a leader, he sets the tempo for the nation by simply believing the Lord's prophet.

It is here that Jehoshaphat turns on the ignition switch to both God's heart, and the heart of His nation. It is here that he teaches us one of the most important lessons about praise, and it is this: **Praise is an act of the will!** It is a decision. You see, there will be times in your life when you will absolutely not feel like praising God. Nevertheless, if you obey God, and do it anyway, regardless of your feelings, you will experience the power of God in your life. The psalmist, David said it best in **Psalm 34:1**, when he proclaimed, **"I will bless the LORD at all times, and his praise shall continually be in my mouth."** In other words, he is saying, "I will myself to bless the Lord, regardless of how I feel!" This is precisely what Jehoshaphat decided to do, which ultimately leads him to one of the greatest victories in biblical history.

On the day of the battle, this great leader stands up before his people and proclaims these great words as recorded in **II Chronicles 20:20**, **"..."Listen to me, Judah and people of Jerusalem! Have faith in the LORD your God and you will be upheld; have faith in his prophets and you will be successful."** What happens next was simply amazing. As Jehoshaphat and his army position themselves, and begin to praise God with all of their might, the angel of the Lord shows and sends the enemies into utter confusion. As the people of God stand still, they begin to see Ammon and Moab attacking Mount Seir, utterly destroying them. Then, in confusion, they begin fiercely to destroy one another until not one person is left alive.

²² **As they began to sing and praise, the LORD set ambushes against the men of Ammon and Moab and Mount Seir who were invading Judah, and they were defeated. ²³ The Ammonites and Moabites rose up against the men from Mount Seir to destroy and annihilate them. After they finished slaughtering the men from Seir, they helped to destroy one another.**

²⁴ **When the men of Judah came to the place that overlooks the desert and looked toward the vast army, they saw only dead bodies lying on the ground; no one had escaped. ²⁵ So Jehoshaphat and his men went to carry off their plunder, and they found among them a great amount of equipment and clothing and also articles of value—more than they could take away. There was so much plunder that it took three days to collect it. ²⁶ On the fourth day they assembled in the Valley of Berakah, where they praised the LORD. This is why it is called the Valley of Berakah to this day.**

²⁷ **Then, led by Jehoshaphat, all the men of Judah and Jerusalem returned joyfully to Jerusalem, for the LORD had given them cause to rejoice over their enemies. ²⁸ They entered Jerusalem and went to the temple of the LORD with harps and lyres and trumpets.**

²⁹ **The fear of God came on all the surrounding kingdoms when they heard how the LORD had fought against the enemies of Israel. 30 And the kingdom of Jehoshaphat was at peace, for his God had given him rest on every side.**

II Chronicles 20:22-29

As a result of praise, not only did Jehoshophat and his people win the battle without having to fight, but the wealth that they took from their enemies was so great, that it took them three days to gather. By simply obeying God's prophet and praising God in the midst of a tough situation, Judah, literally experienced a great wealth transfer overnight! Talk about investments! In essence, they **prospered**. In addition, something equally as great happened. When all of the neighboring kingdoms heard of what happened in this battle, the fear of God fell on them, and God gave Judah rest from their enemies. In other words, they were **established**. This was a result of what Jehoshaphat had previously stood up and spoken to his people beforehand. Just as Jehoshophat and Judah experienced great victory by praising God, when you use the weapon of praise, you will as well.

Implementing the Strategy

7 Tactics to Praise God on the Battlefield

The Jehoshaphat Model

1. **When faced with calamity, decide to seek the wisdom of God first.** When bad news comes, the enemy will try to use fear to paralyze your faith. Jehoshaphat, though afraid, decided to seek God by declaring a fast and prayer. Though he got a bad report, he refused to let fear overtake him.

2. **Listen to God's prophets.** One word from God can change your life forever. When troubles arrive, there will be great distractions by the enemy to not listen to the people of God that are in your life. Your logic, the media, friends, and even family will sometimes try to distract you from listening to your pastor. Because Jehoshaphat listened to Godly counsel, he prospered.

3. **Don't try to do it alone, if you don't have to do so.** God has placed people in your life to help you. The Bible says that if "one can put a thousand to flight, two can put ten thousand to flight." Jehoshaphat solicited the involvement of his nation.

4. **Stand up and lead!** Be bold! Leadership is not optional with God. Not only is God watching you, but so are people! When a leader stands up for God in the face of danger, it infuses faith into God's people. Mark Twain said, "Courage is not the absence of fear, but the mastery of fear."

5. **When praising God, recall former victories or accounts, where God showed himself strong on your behalf.** Jeshoshaphat reminded God of what He had done, and what He was going to do this time. Thank God in advance for the victory!

6. **Be passionate about your praise.** Don't be ashamed to praise God with all of your might! Remember, on one occasion, David danced so hard before his people, that he danced out of his clothes. The people of Judah praised God loudly with all of their might, shouting "Praise the LORD, for His mercy endures forever!" Remember, you are bragging on someone who has never lost a battle. He is worthy to receive all of the bragging you can give.

7. Once you achieve your victory, don't forget to give God the praise continually. Make praising God a lifestyle. Don't forget! One of the things unique about us as human beings is that we tend to have a short memory. The Psalmist says, "I will bless the LORD at all times, and His praise shall continually be in my mouth." Joshua 1:8 says, "Keep this Book of the Law always on your lips; meditate on it day and night, so that you may be careful to do everything written in it. Then you will be prosperous and successful." The people of Judah remembered to thank God after they won their battle. Make sure that you make praise, not an occasion, but a lifestyle.

Praise empowers us to receive God's victory and it prepares the way for God to give it to us.

Now, you have the weapon. How are you going to use it?

Victory is mine! In the next 7 days, I will act on the following in order to Praise God:

_____

_____

_____

_____

Chapter 8

Be Prepared

*"Winning isn't everything,
but the willingness to prepare to win is."*
-Vince Lombardi

*"Suppose one of you wants to build a tower.
Won't you first sit down and estimate the cost to see
if you have enough money to complete it?"*
-Luke 14:28

Weapon #7: Be Prepared

Why It Is Powerful

Being prepared ups the odds and levels the battlefield. To achieve any form of greatness, we must be willing not only to count the cost, but to pay the price. Boy Scouts are known for their simple, yet effective motto, "Be prepared." The Boy Scouts organization is a tremendous organization sending such a powerful message to young men. For those of you who were Scouts, you may remember the day you were dropped off in the woods, given a compass and a few other essentials, and told to find your way back to your point of origin. It wasn't easy, but somehow you made it to your destination.

Even if you were not a Boy Scout, you can incorporate the Boy Scouts' creed of being prepared into your life. Because of the preparation of the Boy Scout, he would be able to navigate the challenges of the woods and find his way. That valuable lesson would teach him the importance of being prepared for any situation. It gave him the confidence to know that if you worked hard up front, it would pay off in the end. It drove home the timeless truth that those who are better prepared to win usually end up the victors.

As a former Boy Scout, I have fond memories of carrying out this creed as a young scout. However, this concept is so neglected in the workforce today. Most people are anything but prepared. After conducting training internationally for several years, I have discovered that preparation and efficiency have been replaced by excuses, blame, and mediocrity. While I can certainly understand that mistakes will happen, it is vital that we accept responsibility for those mistakes. A lack of accepting responsibility has become the great cancer of the twenty-first century. We cannot avoid the fact that if we are ever going to become skillful at anything, we must prepare.

Strategy for Victory

"Seest thou a man that is skillful in his business, he shall stand before kings; He shall not stand before mean men." Proverbs 22:29

Action 1: Ask and Answer the Hard Questions

- What type of preparation are you willing to undergo to achieve your goal?

- What are you willing to sacrifice to realize that dream?

- What unhealthy relationships are you willing to cut off?

- What unproductive habits are you willing to break?

- What mental conditioning are you willing to endure?

These are all valid questions we must ask ourselves before assuming we truly desire something because sometimes we confuse our wants with our desires. It is here that we separate the winners from the losers. When we want something and we do not get it, it may not be a big deal. Desire, however, is much different. When we desire something, we will not stop until we get it. When true desire is present, we find ourselves making any adjustment, correcting any attitude, and enduring any hardship to acquire the goal. Therefore, if we truly desire something, we must be willing to ask ourselves some tough questions and be honest with our answers.

Many look for the easy way out because cheaper dreams require easier efforts. Big dreams require big efforts. Are you a big dreamer?

Action 2: Differentiate Luck from Preparation

There are many people who believe that luck plays a significant role in achieving success. It is common to hear family, friends, and colleagues say that they want something, but act in ways detrimental to their aims. They could want anything from a new car, a promotion, or even marriage. (Do any of these goals sound familiar to you?) Yet, interestingly enough, you never see them realize their goals. What happened?

In many instances, they did not truly count the costs associated with the attainment of the goal. They were not really committed to achieving the goal. They were wishing rather than doing. They were hoping for a little luck.

Philanthropist Peter J. Daniels had this to say about commitment: "Commitment is the willingness to bear pain as a necessary cost toward the benefit." Are you willing to bear the necessary pain to achieve your goal? Or are you depending more on your horoscope, the right conditions, or even luck to achieve your goal? True, it seems that some people get all the breaks. We can begin to think that it must be luck that makes the difference – the kind of luck that must be reserved for only a few – not the rest of us.

However, let's consider the words of a few visionaries. Earl Nightingale said this about luck: "As for luck, forget about it. Luck is what happens when preparedness meets opportunity." Legendary Green Bay Packers football coach, Vince Lombardi proclaimed, "Winning isn't everything, but the willingness to prepare to win is." Finally, James Allen in his classic little book, *As A Man Thinketh*, wrote "Men are willing to improve their circumstances, but are unwilling to improve themselves." Show me a person who is willing to win, and I'll show you a person who is willing to prepare. The real problem in our workforce today is that people talk more about their conditions than they do about their personal responsibility to prepare.

Action 3: Decide What You are Prepared to Do

In the top-rated movie, "The Untouchables," actor Sean Connery, playing the role of Jimmy Malone, a beat cop, poses an unforgettable question to actor Kevin Costner, playing the role of Elliott Ness, the young treasury agent sent to Chicago to take on the mob, headed by Al Capone. It is a question we all must be willing to ask ourselves.

Sean Connery as Malone is a tough, cagey, and seasoned Irishman with a great sense of right and wrong. The city of Chicago has become incredibly corrupted, from its police force, to its judges, to its mayor. Kevin Costner as Ness, a young and naïve treasury agent, is constantly fooled and ridiculed by mob informants within the police force. After a tough day of dejection and depression, Ness meets Malone on the street while walking his beat. Ness then goes to visit the cop at his home to ask for his help in taking down Al Capone. Malone initially says no, not wanting to get involved, but something interesting happens the next day.

Malone shows up at Ness' office in street clothes. Knowing that they need real privacy, Malone takes Ness to a Catholic church. They talk while kneeling at the altar. Malone looks Ness in the eye and asks: "Do you really want to get Al Capone, Mr. Ness? Then, he asks the critical, unforgettable question: You see what I'm asking is, "What are you prepared to do?" Malone wanted to know: Have you counted the cost? Do you know what price you will have to pay to get Al Capone?

Malone was from Chicago, and he knew what treachery these men were willing to perform. He knew that unless Ness was willing to fight fire with fire, he need not even begin to take on Capone, and that once involved there was no turning back. In this classic scene Sean Connery says these lines: "You want to get Capone, here's how you do it. He sends one of your guys to the hospital; you send one of his guys to the morgue. And that's how you get Capone, that's the Chicago way!" Now I certainly don't condone violence of any type. I believe it should be avoided at all costs, to the best of one's ability. However, the odds are that you probably didn't live in Chicago at that time, and you were not facing Al Capone, either. What I want to illustrate here is the level of intensity Ness was going to need in order to be successful at achieving his goal. The stakes were high, but he had to decide what he was prepared to do.

What if more Christians had this level of desire and intensity in the workplace? As Christians we have forgotten that walking in love does not mean that we are to be devoid of intensity, toughness, and passion. Jesus further solidifies this point in **Matthew 11:12** when he proclaims boldly, **"From the days of John the Baptist until now, the Kingdom of Heaven suffereth violence, and the violent take it by force."** Let's ask ourselves: "What am I prepared to do?"

Capone's henchmen go to Jimmy Malone's home to kill him. Outnumbered, Malone is brutally attacked by machine gun fire, but not without a courageous stand. Malone is left bleeding on the floor of his home. Ness arrives, but he is too late. As Malone is dying in Ness's arms, with his body riddled with bullets, he asks again with his last breath, "What are you prepared to do?"

As I close this chapter, I ask you the same question, "What are you prepared to do?"

Implementing the Strategy

7 Tactics to Be Prepared on the Battlefield

1. What special training courses does your employer provide for you to improve your skills? Take advantage of all opportunities to improve yourself.

2. When you think you've done all you can do, think again. Very rarely has anyone done everything they can.

3. What books can you read, CDs can you listen to, or research can you gather online to better improve your skills?

4. Who do you respect or admire that would be willing to mentor you?

5. Spend some time thinking about how you can better provide your services.

6. Taking time to think is one of the most productive activities we can do. It is actually the hardest work of all; that's probably why we do it so little. Think about what you do best and what you want to do better.

7. Read the biographies of great people. Biographies are great because they chronicle the lives of people who overcame insurmountable odds. When you get it in your spirit, it will encourage and inspire you.

Preparation is a constant action. As you continue to do and give your best, don't worry about what comes next. Pray and be confident that God sees your faith and is working on your behalf.

Now, you have the weapon. How are you going to use it?

Victory is mine! In the next 7 days, I will act on the following in order to Be Prepared:

_____

_____

_____

_____

Chapter 9

Seek Wisdom

*"Wisdom is not a product of schooling
but of the lifelong attempt to acquire it."*
-Albert Einstein

*"The beginning of wisdom is this: Get wisdom.
Though it cost all you have, get understanding."*
Proverbs 4:7

Weapon #8: Seek Wisdom

Why It Is Powerful

When I was a boy, my little brother Tracy would do something that would really annoy me. He would ride his tricycle into the wall over and over again. Not only would he do it constantly, but he seemed to derive great joy from it. He was only about five years old at the time. Eventually, he stopped doing it. Tracy is now an adult, forty-six years old at the writing of this book. Suppose at the age of forty-six he still rode his tricycle into the wall as he did when he was five years old? Wouldn't that be abnormal? That's what happens when someone has no wisdom. They continue to make the same mistakes over and over again. Insanity has been described as "doing the same thing repeatedly and expecting a different result." **"The beginning of wisdom is this: Get wisdom. Though it cost all you have, get understanding." (Proverbs 4:7)** Simply put, wisdom is the ability to apply what you know.

According to Henry David Thoreau, "It is characteristic of wisdom not to do desperate things." Solomon, considered by many as the wisest man who ever lived, wrote the aforementioned Proverb. I would imagine that if God said through him that wisdom was principal, it must be vital. For Solomon to write that wisdom was the foremost thing, then we need to everything in our power to obtain it.

Strategy for Victory

The story about my brother may be comical, but hopefully you get the point. How many adults do you know who repeatedly make the same errors? Why is this so? It would seem as if they "would know better," then do better. Yet, no matter how old we are, sometimes we can fall into a pattern of repeating mistakes because we do not exercise wisdom. Here are a few matters to consider in avoiding a life without wisdom.

1. **Pride** – It is okay to admit that some area of our lives may need to be changed, and we cannot be ashamed to do so. Pride is a barrier that does not allow wisdom to penetrate. The best thing for us to do is embrace change. We must humble ourselves to receive wisdom. "Pride goes before destruction, a haughty spirit before a fall." (Proverbs 16:18)

2. **Convenience** – One of the reasons we don't embrace wisdom is because of convenience. It's much more comfortable for us to remain as we are, no matter how wrong we may be. Somehow, we have equated feeling good to being wise or right. Nothing could be farther from the truth. Usually this world's greatest gifts involve pain. For example, I love my son Christian very much, but I have no desire to bear a child myself! I thank the Lord that his mother was willing to accept the immediate pain for the greater joy he would bring later.

3. **Ignorance** – Whenever we do not pay the price on the front end, we do not know the joys on the back end. In order to get something you've never had, you must be prepared to do something you have never done. It takes faith and courage to trust that God knows what is best for you. When you understand the benefit of wisdom, you will embrace it.

4. **Emotion** – One of the greatest hiding places for Satan is in your emotions. When you operate in wisdom you learn that you are not a product of your emotions, but of your choices. How

many times have you heard someone say, "They made me angry!" Is that really true? Who really made you angry? Let me give you one hint, it starts with a "Y." You guessed it, you made you angry.

5. **Offense** – We live in a day and age of what I call, "The Walking Offended." Many people don't really want to hear the truth. They want to have their ears tickled. The moment that they begin to receive constructive feedback about an issue, they become offended. Sometimes we fall victim to human nature. When we hear something we do not like, we immediately become offended, shut down, and miss the information we may need to hear. Be aware. Offense is a tool used by Satan to shut you down and render you unproductive. As scripture states, "A brother wronged is more unyielding than a fortified city; disputes are like barred gates of a citadel." (Proverbs 18:19)

6. **Simplicity** – One of the most shocking reasons people don't receive wisdom is that it simply seems too easy. Because we live in a generation and age of intelligence, common sense is not automatic. Wisdom is not intelligence. Wisdom comes from God. How many people do you know who are "book smart," but lacking greatly in wisdom? I believe that God is really much simpler than we make Him. It takes humility to receive wisdom. Unfortunately many people are blinded by pride and arrogance.

These are just a few of the pitfalls that can stall your journey to wisdom. Hopefully, by now you understand the importance of seeking wisdom. God loves you, and has purchased for you the good life. God has designed a simple plan for you. He wants you to work smarter, rather than harder. He wants you to live a life that is fearless, courageous, and stress free. God wants you to have optimum health, wealth, and relationships. Above all else, God desires for you to fulfill His plan for your life. Wisdom is the key to making that happen.

Implementing the Strategy

7 Tactics to Seek Wisdom on the Battlefield

1. **Study the Word** – Study the Word of God. The Word of God is our instruction manual for successful living, containing life's answers. Read it daily, and see your life soar! It is an

inexhaustible living document which was inspired by God. Joshua 1:8 says, "Keep this Book of the Law always on your lips; meditate on it day and night, so that you may be careful to do everything written in it. Then you will be prosperous and successful." This scripture referring to the Word is the only place where success is mentioned in the Bible.

2. **Study the Words** – Become informed. We need to know the Word, but God desires that His people be informed. Hosea 4:6 says, "My people are destroyed from lack of knowledge." We are living in the "Information Age." Orville Ray Wilson said, "Information is the currency of the 21st century." Do you know everything there is to know about your profession? How about where your elected officials stand on political issues? In the day in which we live, whoever wins the information race usually wins the overall race.

3. **Prayer** – Prayer and fellowship with God is one of the greatest ways of gaining wisdom. When you spend time with and communicate with God, you begin to tap into God's ways and wisdom. Problems at work can only be solved at the core by prayer. When you pray to God, you tap into God's infinite intelligence. God desires to talk to you. Will you talk to God?

4. **Church and Bible Study Attendance** – Being taught God's Word is crucial in obtaining wisdom. There are anointed men and women of God who are skilled at teaching God's Word. I thank God for my pastor's gift for teaching the Word as it relates to wisdom. Through simplicity and understanding, he creates a hunger and thirst for wisdom. We can't wait to come to church. Some people may say, "You don't really have to go to church!" They are right. You don't, depending on what you want. However, if you want to gain wisdom, it would be a good idea. We should open ourselves to receive knowledge from others who have the gift for teaching and the grace from God to do so.

5. **Experience** – Experience garners wisdom. Ideally, we would all like to learn without making any mistakes. Unfortunately, that is not the way it always happens. I do think, however, that we should learn from our mistakes and determine not to make the same ones repeatedly. Some of life's greatest successes come from failing first. Thomas Edison reportedly failed at least 3,000 times before inventing the light bulb. When you do fail, determine to get up smarter than before the fall.

6. Learn From Other People's Successes and Failures – One of the great ways to gain wisdom is to study the lives of great men and women of God. Many great people have noted that reading biographies helped them to become successful. Study what makes people great and what makes people not so great. Some people teach us what not to do. Determine to learn from them, as well.

7. Speak God's Word Over your Life – Your mouth is a powerful weapon! Speak God's word over your life daily. Write down scriptures that say what God said about you and say them over your life daily. Joshua 1:8 says that the word should not depart from out of your mouth. That means that you should only say what God says about you according to scripture. Confess daily that you have the wisdom of God. Make a decision to never speak negative words about yourself or others.

Wisdom: Far Greater than Intelligence

Let me offer one final note on seeking wisdom. Regardless of our education, background, or upbringing we can all tap into infinite intelligence through the wisdom of God. Often, when we see others making the same error repeatedly, we feel compelled to alert them that they are doing wrong. Yet, it almost seems inevitable that they will respond, "I know that!" They may have several degrees, and may even possess a rich library of interesting books. Sound familiar? Stephen Covey, author of the *7 Habits of Highly Effective People* said this: "To know to do, and not do, is to not know." If that person had really understood the principle, the conversation would be unnecessary. Determine to be teachable.

The previous illustration is an example of someone who is intelligent, but has no wisdom. When you have wisdom, you finally get it. You apply what you know. When someone has wisdom, he or she should be the most productive person at the company because they will tap into a knowledge base that even extraordinarily intelligent people cannot. Wise people will perform at levels that will confound natural laws and reasoning. For example, when you fully yield yourself to seek wisdom through God, an employer would rather do anything than let you go! Remember there were many talented astrologers in Joseph's day, but only Joseph had the solution for preserving Egypt, his family, and indeed, the world.

Now, you have the weapon. How are you going to use it?

Victory is mine! In the next 7 days, I will act on the following in order to Seek Wisdom:

_____

_____

_____

_____

Chapter 10

Take Aim

"If you aim at nothing, you'll probably hit it."

-Tim Hansel

*"I press toward the mark for the prize
of the high calling of God in Christ Jesus."*

-Philippians 3:14

Weapon #9: Take Aim

Why It Is Powerful

If we are to be truly productive and successful in life, it is imperative that we take aim. By taking aim, I mean that we set goals for our lives, and make definite, deliberate plans to be successful. We live our lives either by design or default. When we live our lives by design, we empower ourselves to be successful on purpose. When we live our lives by default, we empower other people and circumstances to determine our success.

Goals create a deliberate path for success. The clearer our target, the better our chances are of hitting it. Such is the case with goal setting. Have you ever wondered why people who have goals tend to achieve them? "Ready, aim, fire" is a military order barked by a military commander to soldiers preparing to attack. The command means position your weapon so that you can hit your target before firing it. By taking aim, we greatly increase our chances of hitting our target and defeating our enemy. It is amazing what we can achieve by simply aiming and trying.

Can you imagine what would happen if a soldier never took the time to aim before firing his or her weapon? Essentially these soldiers would be turned into loose cannons. More specifically, four significant things would likely happen if we failed to take aim before firing:

1. We could injure or destroy ourselves, which is the enemy's ultimate plan. Subsequently, the enemy wins by forfeit.

2. We could injure or destroy our fellow soldiers, or those who God has assigned to help us. Have you ever damaged a God-ordained relationship by breaking a commitment, simply because you didn't plan? The result is that we sometimes are not fighting the enemy, but each other. All of this could happen, simply because we refused to plan.

3. We could injure or destroy our loved ones. How many relationships have been broken or damaged because of bad planning or goal setting? Sometimes it starts with smaller issues and then mushrooms into larger ones. How many husbands have forgotten their marriage anniversaries or the like by failing to plan?

4. Finally, the enemy doesn't really have to defeat us, because we do a pretty good job of defeating ourselves. Like Sampson walking around blind with gouged out eyes, we fall as easy prey to the enemy.

The revered American educator and clergyman, Dr. Benjamin E. Mays had much to say about goal setting. Dr. Mays was president of Morehouse College while Dr. Martin Luther King, Jr. was a student. This great man, who is credited with teaching the young King to dream, said this about goals:

"It must be borne in mind that the tragedy of life does not lie in not reaching your goal. The tragedy of life lies in having no goal to reach. It isn't a disgrace not to reach the stars, but it is a disgrace to have no stars to reach for."

The tragedy today is that we are just like the soldier with the weapon, who refuses to take aim. By failing to set goals and plan, we are failing to realize that failing to plan is planning to fail. We hurt ourselves greatly, but in many instances the people who are hurt the most are our families and loved ones. As a result, we continually miss the mark and we miss out on many good things in life as well.

Strategy for Victory

Action 1: Claim Your Birthright as a Goal Setter

According to Aristotle, "Humankind is a teleological organism." We are born with a purpose in mind. We were created by a God of order and design with a specific plan for our lives. Because God is a planner, and we were made in His image, that same planning mechanism lives in us. Not only were we given an innate desire to set goals, we are literally goal-setting creatures. We were not born to flounder through life. We were born with a divine purpose and an expected outcome or end. **Jeremiah 29:11** expresses this tenet beautifully by saying, **"For I know the thoughts that I think toward you, saith the Lord, thoughts of peace, and not evil, to give you an expected end."**

Unlike other creatures, we were born for a unique purpose in life. We were born with a God-ordained gift to both fulfill others and ourselves. Have you ever noticed a person who knows who they are? When people understand their purpose, they are the most fulfilled and satisfied beings on earth. They tend to be more graceful and fully functional because they are operating in the manner for which they were created. Even though they may not have all of the money that they want, they find joy in pursuing their passion. When you're in your purpose, even if tribulation comes, there is an assuring, abiding peace inside of you.

Action 2: Activate Your Inner Goal-Seeking Mechanism (RAS)

Have you ever considered God's handiwork? Have you ever noticed the beauty of the mountains, the wonder of a sunset, or even the synchronicity of wildlife? All of these wonders make it ridiculous to imagine that something else besides God created them. Another one of God's wonders is your Reticular Activating System (RAS). This system, located at the based of your skull, is a built-in goal seeking mechanism, designed for your success. God has literally wired you for success.

Have you ever decided that you wanted a new car and noticed that every car you see is the car you have decided to buy? Where did that notion come from? Your Reticular Activating System. This built-in mechanism, located near your cerebral cortex, doesn't work until you decide on a goal. Once you set a goal, it works in radar-like form to bring into your existence everything you need for the attainment of your goal. The thing that trips the switch of the system is simply your decision or goal.

The Reticular Activating System works this way. Imagine walking though a loud airport. As you stroll, you hear hundreds, perhaps thousands of people talking. Suddenly, an announcement thunders across the PA system. Instantly, your mind zeros in on the message, drowning out all of the background noise irrelevant to the message. This amazing system works as a filter between your conscious and subconscious mind. It takes information from your conscious, and transfers it to your subconscious. The unique thing about your conscious and your subconscious mind is that while your conscious mind operates in reality, your subconscious cannot differentiate between the real and the imagined. The subconscious doesn't discriminate, but rather it simply obeys what you tell it. Because of this feature, you can program it for your success.

Here are some ways to engage your Reticular Activating System for success:

1. **Set a Goal** – Decide on the something you'd like to achieve. This trips the success switch and activates the system.

2. **Visualization** – See yourself achieving or in possession of your desired goal. In your mind's eye envision the successful you. As you imagine, so shall you become! It's important to combine your thoughts with emotion.

3. **Confessions** – Repeat to yourself over and over what you will achieve. Some call these affirmations, but I prefer the term confession, because you're basing it on scripture. The key here is to combine it with scripture. What truly gives confession power is that you are agreeing with what God says about you.

Ensure that you are not confessing anything that is not based on the word of God. God will not bless impure motives. Write down scripture references that validate and confirm what you're confessing. You will be amazed at what God does.

4. Meditation – Keep your goal fixed in your mind at all times. This is why ensuring that your desires are Godly and worthwhile is key. By aligning your goals with God's, you're meditating on the Word and your goals at the same time. Whatever you hold in your mind long enough has to manifest itself.

Author Tim Hansel gives a great example of Reticular Activating System in his book *You Gotta Keep Dancin'*. In this insightful book Hansel tells the story of a man who promised his wife he was going to add a sunroom onto their house. He had been procrastinating for a few reasons:

1. He didn't want to spend the money for the brick.

2. He wasn't quite sure how to do it. (And like most men he didn't want to admit it!)

3. He didn't know where to look.

He then just makes the decision to act. He gets in his car and begins to drive. A few minutes later, he passes a building being torn down. Any idea what the building was made of? You guessed it! Brick! In shock, he keeps on driving. All of a sudden he passes the Kingdome football stadium, which is being demolished. Guess what it was made from? Brick! He had been driving by both of them for months, but had never noticed them. The minute he set the goal, his Reticular Activating System zeroed in on all the things he needed to make the goal a reality. He decided to act, and the sunroom was built at a fraction of the cost.

Implementing the Strategy

7 Tactics to Take Aim on the Battlefield

1. **Set the goal.** Don't wait until you have all of the answers. The answer and resources will come as you act.

2. **Use the S-M-A-R-T formula for goal-setting.** Make sure each
   goal has these five qualities:

   S–pecific

   M–easurable

   A–ction oriented

   R–ealistic

   T–ime bound

3. **Write down the five most important things you need to
   do tomorrow.** As you complete the tasks check them off.
   Remember a goal that is not recorded is a wish.

4. **Have a back-up plan. Always have Plan B ready.** Being
   unprepared will slow down your progress. Keep moving toward
   your goals.

5. **Surround yourself with people who have goals of their own.**
   Likes tend to attract. If you aim at nothing, you will certainly
   hit it.

6. **Confess your goal. Talk about your goals.** Confess them
   out loud. Use the 4 P's of goal affirmations. They should be
   PERSONAL, PRESENT-TENSE, POSITIVE, and PASSIONATE. For
   example: "I am living in my dream home and greatly enjoying
   my life in Atlanta, Georgia by 1/1/11."

7. **Stay inspired.** Create the right inspirational environment
   for goal achievement. What inspires you? Quotes? Music?
   Movies? Books? Church? Whatever is right for you, keep in the
   inspirational juices flowing.

Although your goals may seem intimidating to you, and maybe
even to others, God has wired you for success. When you simply
decide to set a goal, all of heaven backs you up with its resources.

Now, you have the weapon. How are you going to use it?

Victory is mine! In the next 7 days, I will act on the following in order to Take Aim:

_____

_____

_____

_____

Chapter 11

Be Extra-Ordinary

"A change is brought about because ordinary people do extraordinary things."
-President Barack Obama

"If anyone forces you to go one mile, go with them two miles."
-Matthew 5:41

Weapon #10: Be Extra-Ordinary

Why It Is Powerful

In order for us to truly separate ourselves from the crowd, we must become "Extra-ordinary." We must up the "WOW" factor in our performance. The only difference between extraordinary and ordinary is that little extra. We must be willing, not only to do our jobs, but to do extra as well. How few companies or even people go the extra mile in our society today? As Christians, our lives should reflect anything, but usual, ordinary, or regular. In fact, God described us as peculiar people. Because God is a God of excellence, we were created with God's own extra-ordinary DNA. He used no ordinary ingredients and spared no expense in equipping us with greatness. Being extra-ordinary is not a new concept. In fact, Jesus had something profound to say about being extra-ordinary in **Matthew 5:41-42: "If anyone forces you to go one mile, go with them two miles. Give to the one who asks you, and do not turn away from the one who wants to borrow from you."**

In this tremendous passage of scripture, Jesus introduces a new way of thinking that contradicts the normal or ordinary. Countless times in the passage, Jesus says: "You have heard it hath been said... But I say unto you." In using this expression, Jesus is attempting to get his listeners to make a paradigm shift. He desires for them to change from an old, stale way of thinking, to a fresh and better one. What a tremendous, timeless concept! Though almost two thousand years old, being extra-ordinary could revolutionize many of today's struggling organizations caught in a state of complacency.

Strategy for Victory

Giving A Little Extra

WMP Q&A:

Q: What is it that helps us leap to the front of the pack and secure our spot on any roster? What is it that causes us to prosper in any recession?

A: You guessed it! We've got to give that little extra.

How many times have you seen great contests decided only by small margins? Maybe a basketball team wins a game dramatically, by only one point, or a golfer by only a stroke. Perhaps a football team wins the game at the last second by simply kicking a field goal. There is an interesting thing that happens when we witness a team or individual win in this fashion. The extra things that we saw them do to win the contest only tell half of the story. For every little extra thing we see, there are a thousand little extra things they did beforehand that we did not see. We did not see all of the hours of extra training and preparation; the mental conditioning; dieting; and all of the times the team had to play with pain. All of these marvelous extra ingredients created the victory!

One of the best illustrations of being extra-ordinary is an Olympic sprinter. These tremendously well-conditioned athletes are trained to lean their bodies upon approaching the finish line to make and break records of speed – to bring an Olympic medal home. There are three medals given for the three fastest times in the event. Can you guess what amount of time typically separates a gold medal winning finish from a fourth place finish? Hundredths or even thousandths of a second! It is the extra-ordinary effort that separates winners from the losers, and the legendary from the lackadaisical. Have you ever heard the expression, it's the little foxes that spoil the vine? If that's true, then it's the little extra effort that kills the little foxes.

One of the greatest benefits from doing the extra is that many little extras add up to bigger margins. Even when two teams or two athletes play fairly even games, such as soccer or tennis matches, there will eventually be a clear winner. What happens? A lot of little extras come into play. Perhaps someone made an extra block. Possibly, there was extra focus to ensure that penalties were effectively forced. Maybe the extra effort caused a player to gain an extra yard. All of those things worked together to form the winning effort.

As people of God, making the extra effort causes great things to work for us as well. In fact, **Romans 8:28** says, **"All things work together for the good of those who love God, who are called according to His purposes."** I have read this scripture many times in my life, and have not until recently understood the meaning. I don't wish to limit the interpretation, because I think the Word of God is pregnant as it has multiple meanings. However, here is my interpretation in regard to giving a little extra. As long as you love God and are seeking to follow God with all of your heart, things will work together for good. In other words, you don't have to live your life worrying about making mistakes. They will happen! You don't have to spend all of your time trying to be perfect. You cannot succeed at that task. Instead, focus on loving God, seeking God's ways, and doing your BEST! When you mess up, you will, 'fess up and repent. When you do that in sincerity of heart, things tend to all come together beautifully. There is a grace and power over doing your best. God loves you for trying!

Implementing the Strategy

7 Tactics to Be Extra-Ordinary on the Battlefield

1. **Decide to develop and maintain a positive attitude at all times.** Often, the difference between ordinary and extraordinary performance lies in your attitude. Decide to make kindness and smiling a part of your necessary daily garments.

2. **Go the extra mile.** Napoleon Hill in his classic book, *Think and Grow Rich*, listed going the extra mile as one of his key success principles. This concept was not a Hill original. It actually came from Jesus Christ. In Matthew 5:41 Jesus exclaims: "If anyone forces you to go one mile, go with them two miles." In a day and age where average is the norm, this principle sets you apart from the competition.

3. **Become an expert in your field.** Seek to acquire all of the information that you can to become the best in your field of study. Information is power. To quote Orville Ray Wilson, "Information is the currency of the 21st century." With the advent of the Internet, you have advantages available today that were not available before. Let your work speak louder than your mouth.

4. **Under promise and over deliver.** Only make promises that you can keep, and always deliver more than you promise. Never break a promise. One of the major reasons people tend to break promises is over commitment, due to poor planning. It is far better to not make a commitment and keep it, than to make a large commitment and break it.

5. **Anticipate needs and act.** To quote the famous Nike slogan, "Just do it!" If you have to do so, ask. Sometimes people are shy. Be assertive! If you see a need, jump in and fill it without even being asked. To quote Mike Murdock, "People are paid for the problems they solve." Are you solving someone's problem?

6. **Don't take it personal.** In your quest to be extra-ordinary, chances are good to excellent that someone will rub you the wrong way. Sometimes their style may be different than yours. Sometimes you might not have built a high enough level of trust with them, yet. Make it a point to never take it personal. Many times it has nothing to do with you. Never get offended. Choose rather to let it build your character.

7. **Be flexible.** Adapt to necessary changes. One of the greatest values that anyone can bring to the table today is flexibility. Be pliable and adaptable to different situations. Roll with the punches and never get thrown into a tailspin by things that might come up. Be prepared ahead of time and make the adjustment.

It is always interesting to read biographies or watch documentaries about he lives of famous athletes or performers who did enough little extra things to become extra-ordinary. These great feats of fortitude and fearlessness may have been unconventional at times, but they worked. We have the same capacity as "famous" people to be extra-ordinary, too. We can do it with God's help.

Now, you have the weapon. How are you going to use it?

Victory is mine! In the next 7 days, I will act on the following in order to Become Extra-Ordinary:

_____

_____

_____

_____

Chapter 12

Decide To Become Legendary

"We should set out to do our life's work so well that the living, the dead, or the unborn, couldn't do it better."

-Dr. Martin Luther King, Jr.

"And whatsoever ye do, do it heartily, as to the Lord, and not unto men."

-Colossians 3:23

Weapon #11: Decide to Become Legendary

Why It Is Powerful

Once, while attending a customer service seminar in Las Vegas, a slide came across the screen that hit me like a ton of bricks. It featured a slogan Sam Walton created when he founded the Wal-Mart shopping chain. What was this great phrase? "To have customer service that is legendary." Sam Walton made a decision, not just to go into business merely to have a chain of stores. He wanted to create customer service that was so great that it would be the topic of discussion at customers' dinner tables. He decided to do something great. Just as Sam Walton made the decision to do something that was legendary, we should decide to live lives that are legendary. The following poem by Doug Maloch says it best.

Be the Best of Whatever You Are

If you can't be a pine on the top of a hill

Be a scrub in the valley, but be the best little scrub
on the side of the hill

Be a bush if you can't be a tree,

If you can't be a bush be a bit of the grass

And some highway happier make.

If you can't be a muskie, then just be a bass,

But the liveliest bass in the lake.

We can't all be captains, we've got to be crew,

There's something for all of us here.

There's big work to do and there's lesser work, too,

And the thing we must do is the near

If you can't be a highway, then just be a trail.

If you can't be the sun, be a star.

It isn't by size that you win or you fail.

Be the best of whatever you are.

You were born to do something that you and you alone can do better than anyone. When God created you, He placed a unique gift in you to bless humankind. What is that thing that you enjoy doing so well that it's almost as effortless as inhaling? What is the one special gift that you have that meets someone's need, or solves someone's problem? Is there one thing that you do so well that you have developed a reputation for it? We should do everything in our power to prepare to get to that place. It is in this place that we will find our peace, prosperity, joy, and fulfillment.

WMP Q&A:

Q: How many people in our society lead mediocre lives because they never make the decision to be the best at something?

They lead daily routines that are more like rituals of regularity rather than decisions of destiny. They have lost their zest and zeal for life because they have not valued the great duty and privilege of service and giving back to God and humankind for the gifts that we have been given. Why is this the case in our society today?

A: Part of the reason for this is that people have lost faith in God. Employers, corporations, managers, and people have disappointed them. Subsequently, they have justified themselves by not giving their best effort. They have placed more trust and security in these systems and people than they have in God. In turn, they have stopped trusting that God is not only able to bless them, but willing. I would like to pause here for a moment and say that I can certainly understand that there will be hurts in life. We have all endured disappointments in life. However, it's vitally important that our focus stays on God as our source, and not on people.

When people start trusting systems rather than God, they begin to blame God for an unfulfilled life. They fail to recognize that the problem seldom lies with the manufacturer, but with the product. By taking this route – refusing to give their best - they are failing to realize that they are only hurting and robbing themselves. Life was not meant to be lived this way. We were born for something much higher than mediocrity. We were created for greatness.

Strategy for Victory

In order for us to change the pattern of mediocrity as a way of life, we must create a new paradigm. We must begin to see ourselves differently. We must decide to be great and see ourselves as great. I have a little phrase that I like to say and it is this: "The me I see, is the me I'll be." We must throw off past pictures of our failures and embrace the new winner that is hidden deep within us. When we begin to change the person on the inside, we will inevitably begin to see the results on the outside. When we decide to be the best, something great is awakened within us. There is a dignity and honor that causes us to stand taller and feel better about ourselves because we are acting in the manner God created us to act.

God is a creator and a builder of sorts. Since we were created in God's image and likeness, we are builders as well. Since God is a

God of excellence, there is something inside of us that wants to do a good job. When we do, God is pleased because we are imitating Him. Many have asked, "What do I do if I'm working on a job that is not my calling?" Or they might ask, "What if I absolutely hate my job? What do I do in the meantime? How can I know what my calling is or even how to get there?" I think one would have to agree that these are all very good questions. The answer can be found in **Proverbs 16:3** as it reads, **"Commit thy works unto the LORD, and thy thoughts will be established."** In other words, be diligent and excellent at what your hands find to do now, and God will direct you to your destination. Your excellence will spring you into your destiny.

Consider the life of Jesus. He was born to redeem humankind by His ministry and crucifixion at Calvary. Yet, for the majority of His life, He was known as the "Carpenter from Galilee." Get the picture? He spent time developing His skills as an excellent carpenter to set an example to others and to prepare for His ministry. His work as a carpenter made him no less a savior than He was. His trade did not determine who He was, His calling did.

The important thing to note here is that God is all about integrity and character development. He examines our hearts to see if we will be faithful where we are, before advancing to the next level. He loves us enough to ensure that we are ready for the opportunities that are placed before us. The Apostle Paul made tents for a living. I have no doubt that he was a great tentmaker. Yet, he wrote most of the New Testament. Peter was a fisherman by trade. In fact, he was solemnly referred to as the "Big Fisherman." Yet Jesus told him: "Henceforth, ye shall catch men." Catch people is precisely what he did, winning 3,000 souls to Christ at Pentecost. The great evangelist, Billy Graham was a Fuller Brush salesman, and through that significant experience, he learned to sell the Gospel of Jesus Christ to millions.

The Strategy at Work: The Berry Gordy Story

A more modern example of this precept is legendary, record tycoon and founder of Motown Records, Berry Gordy. Born in Detroit, Michigan to self-employed parents, Gordy dropped out of high school at the age of seventeen to pursue a career as a flyweight boxer. Although young Gordy performed well, winning twelve out of fifteen Golden Glove matches, he was drafted to serve in the Korean War, and his boxing career was brought to an end.

Gordy would never forget the dedication, persistence, and desire that he learned from being a fighter, and it would later serve him well.

Upon returning from the war, he purchased a record store with his earnings. Gordy loved music. He would often catch himself at work singing, while listening to the sounds of jazz greats Charlie Parker and Thelonious Monk. Though his love for music was intense, Gordy's inventory would be influenced more by his musical tastes than that of his customers. New names, like Fats Domino were now the craze, and subsequently the store soon closed. Although Gordy would fail in this endeavor, he learned a valuable lesson about supply and demand.

Soon, he landed a job as a chrome trimmer on the assembly line at Ford Motor Company. The assembly line process was amazing to behold for Gordy. He would observe things like the quality control department, which tested to insure that the quality of the product was optimum. What was most astonishing to him was the fact that all of these processes came from one man's vision. Although the process was monotonous, Gordy would learn it well and become excellent at it. To avoid the monotony, he would sing songs while he worked. He realized that he could either focus on the monotony or on his love for music. It helped him, and made the time go by faster.

Then, an interesting thing happened. Gordy began to write songs in his head. He quickly realized that the songs were good, and he was able to sell them to Decca Records, who paid him handsomely for his songs. It wasn't long before Gordy's spare time hobby was generating more income than his assembly line job. Local singers began to sing his songs, and Gordy soon developed a reputation as songwriter, but writing songs wasn't enough.

Like Sam Walton, Gordy had a vision of becoming legendary. He didn't want to merely make records. He had something much bigger in mind: Mass Production. Gordy wanted to turn his record company into the Ford Motor Company of the music industry. Ford had become famous, not for inventing the automobile, but for mass producing it with the assembly line process. Gordy had an idea: What if he could mass produce hit records in the same manner that Ford produced automobiles? What would happen if he could assemble the best talent in America and produce a sound that would take America by storm?

Gordy realized that this was his vision and quickly acted. At the suggestion of his young singer and protégé, William "Smoky" Robinson, Gordy borrowed $700 from his father and purchased Motown Records. Hit records began to pour out of Motown as African American artists and groups were discovered daily. Artists such as The Temptations, The Supremes, Marvin Gaye, and the Jackson 5 were ruling the charts. The Motown sound had become

a reality, producing more hit records at one time than any other
record company in history. Gordy's dream of becoming legendary
had become a reality. Everything in his life had prepared him for this
destiny.

What if Gordy had not worked at Ford? What if he had shirked his
responsibilities on the assembly line or decided that this work was
beneath him? I believe that he never would have realized the creation
of Motown. Gordy produced a genre and generation of music that
crossed all cultural lines and shaped the culture of the world as we
know it. Songs like "Ain't No Mountain High Enough," "Baby Love,"
and "My Girl" have built bridges of unity, love, and joy. The sound,
effect, and influence of Motown were so great, that the name Motown
will live forever in the hearts and minds of people all over the world.
As a result of his vision and decision to become legendary, Gordy will
be forever remembered as the man that created Motown. For what
will you be remembered?

Legendary People and How They Are Remembered

- King David - "The King"

- Muhammad Ali - "The Champ"

- John Wooten- "The Wizard of Westwood"

- The Wright Brothers- "Inventors of Flight"

- Dr. Martin Luther King, Jr.- "The Civil Rights Movement"

- Michael Jordan- "Air Jordan"

- Michael Jackson-"The King of Pop"

- Elvis Presley- "The King of Rock 'n Roll"

- Henry Ford- "Mass Producer of the Automobile"

- Thomas Edison- "Inventor of the Light Bulb"

- Winston Churchill- "Deliverer and Inspiration of Great Britain"

- Shirley Chisholm- "First African American Woman to Run for
  President of the United States."

- Harriet Tubman- "Leader of the Underground Railroad."

Implementing the Strategy

7 Tactics to Declare "I Am Legend" on the Battlefield

1. Pray and ask God for wisdom and direction in following your calling. Expect to hear from God, and be willing to obey God, regardless of the instructions.

2. Begin today to invest the time and effort to perform tasks in an excellent manner. Determine to do tasks well, regardless of how challenging. Excellence breeds excellence.

3. Begin to reflect upon your life and your gifts. Even inquire of those you respect and admire about the things that they feel you are gifted in.

4. Develop a plan for your transition. Write down a strategy for making it happen. If you are currently working in a different field, perhaps you can use the weekends to develop your gift. The key is to determine an amount of time you will invest and stay with it.

5. Determine the people and resources that you will need to attain your goal. Is it money you need? Perhaps favor, resources, or relationships can open doors that money cannot. Make a decision and go for it!

6. Act! Focus your energies on the attainment of your life's work. Eliminate the distractions of people and activities that are counterproductive and take you away from your goal. Decide to work tirelessly and intelligently until your dream is achieved.

7. Begin to see yourself as great! Choose someone that you admire as a role model. Begin to model leadership behavior. Visualize! When you go to the movies, envision yourself as the hero. Study the lives of the great. Here is a great quote to use for inspiration by Henry Wadsworth Longfellow: "The lives of great men (and women) remind us all that our lives can be sublime, and departing, leave behind our footprints on the sands of time."

Never be afraid to become legendary. An awesome God did not create us to be mediocre. Be the best where you are to prepare to be the legend you were created to be.

The following poem by Marianne Williamson says it best:

Our Greatest Fear

It is our light not our darkness that most frightens us.
Our deepest fear is not that we are inadequate.
Our deepest fear is that we are powerful beyond measure.
It is our light not our darkness that most frightens us.
We ask ourselves, who am I to be brilliant, gorgeous,
talented and fabulous?

Actually, who are you not to be?
You are a child of God.
Your playing small does not serve the world.
There's nothing enlightened about shrinking so that other
people won't feel insecure around you.

We were born to make manifest the glory of
God that is within us.

It's not just in some of us; it's in everyone.
And as we let our own light shine,
we unconsciously give other people
permission to do the same.

As we are liberated from our own fear,
Our presence automatically liberates others.

—Marianne Williamson

Now, you have the weapon. How are you going to use it?

Victory is mine! In the next 7 days, I will act on the following in
order to Become Legendary:

_____

_____

_____

_____

Chapter 13

Endeavor

*"If one advances confidently in the direction of [their]
dreams and endeavors to live the life which [they]have imagined,
[they] will meet with a fate unexpected in common hours."*

-Henry David Thoreau

*Diligent hands will rule,
but laziness ends in forced labor.*

-Proverbs 12:24

Weapon #12: Endeavor

Why It Is Powerful

Philosopher Henry David Thoreau declared, "I know of no more
encouraging fact than the unquestionable ability of [human beings]
to elevate [their lives] by conscious endeavor." To endeavor simply
means to make the effort; to try or to strive; to determine to stay with
it and not give up.

Many people find themselves leading unproductive, unfulfilled
lives because they simply do not try that thing or passion that will
bring them joy. Even the best laid plans are destined to fail without the
corresponding effort. There is something beautiful and pure about

working hard in a determined, resolved fashion. It is as if God's power is released when we use what we have. William Ellery Channing wrote, "A man [or woman] in earnest finds means, or, if he [or she] cannot find, creates them. A vigorous purpose makes much out of little, breathes power into weak instruments, disarms difficulties, and even turns them into assistances. Every condition has means of progress, if we have spirit enough to use them."

Strategy for Victory

Now that you have examined eleven weapons of mass production, you must stop here and ask: "Am I really committed to my goal? Have I counted the costs?" Jesus speaks of this concept in **Luke 14:28, "Suppose one of you wants to build a tower. Won't you first sit down and estimate the cost to see if you have enough money to complete it?**

In addition to assessing your commitment and counting the costs, it is important to have a clear understanding of how the enemy works. By design, there will be intentional diversions whenever we decide to be productive for God. Satan knows that if he can outlast us and wear us out, we will become frustrated and quit. Distractions will come in all shapes and sizes as warfare against you in your worthy pursuit. You will likely experience them in the form of everything from negative attitudes, jealousy, and even well-meaning relatives, as did Jesus. Are you prepared to deal with the pressures of mediocrity and accept the fact that it won't be easy? These are important questions that should be asked in order to give you proper perspective.

One of the best examples of the power of endeavor is the Space Shuttle appropriately named the "Endeavor." I like it because it so well illustrates God's mission and purpose for our lives. What an awesome thing the launching of the shuttle is to behold. When the shuttle lifts off, there is an incredible amount of power and thrust to lift the massive craft from the earth's gravitational pull into orbit. Have you ever watched a takeoff? The shuttle launch is a tremendous spectacle of fire, steel, and smoke. Amazingly, the majority of fuel used throughout the shuttle's entire flight is expended during the first few minutes of the launch. Once a rocket breaks free of earth's atmosphere it glides almost effortlessly through space. Our lives as

Christians are in many ways very similar to that of the space shuttle. If we launch our lives with the thrust of God's mission and purpose, we will overcome the pull of mediocrity, and glide through the call God has ordained for us.

However, without the will to use the weapon of endeavor, whenever we attempt to climb, there are multiple encumbrances and distractions trying to hold us down or detour our route. Some of them will be people that the enemy has assigned to your life. Some of them will be circumstances that attempt to buffet you so that you will get frustrated and throw in the towel. Setbacks can even come in the form of past failures and negative experiences. These experiences are designed to make you bitter about life, so that you will live in the past instead of facing the future. If we are to be true Mass Producers, it is important that we put the past in perspective. Motivational speaker, Willie Jollie said it best when he proposed, "The past should be a place of reference, not residence." In other words, it is alright to look at the past from a perspective of reflection, but we shouldn't just camp out there.

As long as Satan can keep you in the past, you will never dream or focus on the great plans that God has for your life.

WMP Q&A:

Q: "How can I overcome this incredible pull of mediocrity?

A: Colossians 3:1 "Since, then, you have been raised with Christ, set your hearts on things above, where Christ is, seated at the right hand of God." Seek those things that are Godly and higher, then your life will also rise higher.

You see there are many tools that Satan will use to hold you down and contain you. Some of them are actually things that are intended for good. However, what may seem to be good, may not necessarily be God. God is not interested in your settling for less than the best. God has your best in mind. It is only in seeking God's best that we can experience the great freedom and liberty that God has designed for us. Only then can we glide.

A great example of breaking free from an encumbrance that may have been good for you once is in the classic movie "Forrest Gump." Young Forrest is encumbered by steel braces on his legs, which are used to help him walk. He is more stilted than a rusty Tin Man in "The Wizard of Oz." In one memorable scene, when bullies chase Forrest, with all of his might, he runs for his life. Although Forrest extends every effort to outpace the bullies, it appears that his capture is eminent. Yet, just when it seems that he is about to be caught, an amazing thing happens. As his childhood friend Jennie screams, "Run Forrest, run," his braces break off his legs.

Ironically, the lack of support doesn't slow Forrest down. In fact, he is now capable of outrunning his bike-riding pursuers. His legs are healed. In a burst of poetic euphoria, he experiences the freedom of running in wide open fashion. The braces, once used to straighten him up, had become an encumbrance, but never again would he be held back by them. Forrest had discovered that he could not only run, but run fast. His new love of running would take him to the University of Alabama as an all-American football player and around the world as a celebrity. In the film, Forrest Gump becomes a household name. I love this movie because it is the story that God has designed for all of our lives. In addition to breaking free from such an encumbrance, Forrest had a set of simple principles, taught to him by his mother, and he followed them. In doing so, he became great. Forrest Gump endeavored to live a purposeful life by overcoming great obstacles.

Like Forrest Gump, we, too, have been given a simple set of principles recorded in a book called the Bible. These principles were designed by God so that we could experience abundant life. When we follow them, we soon discover that great things happen for us. Likewise, by imitating the space shuttle, and making the effort to climb higher, God empowers us to break away from the weights that hold us down. You were created to soar, not to meander, my friend.

Implementing the Strategy

7 Tactics to Endeavor on the Battlefield

1. Prayer

2. Accountability and Right Relationships

3. Study of God's Word

4. Faith

5. Love

6. Preparation

7. Persistence and Diligence

Finally, I will offer one more illustration of flight to emphasize the power of endeavor. The bald eagle is a majestic bird symbolizing strength, grace, and freedom. Unlike most birds, the eagle does not flock with others. Instead, it opts to attack the dangers of the world on its own. Because of its amazing respiratory system, it flies at uncommon altitudes that would kill other birds. If other birds tried to follow it, they would fall out of the sky like flies. God has designed you to be like that eagle. Fly high toward the sun, when others are walking around like chickens or hanging around dead things like buzzards. You will notice that when you decide to seek higher things, others will not be able to fly as high as you.

How many of you have decided to fly higher by not choosing to gossip? Did you notice how unpopular you became all of a sudden? Or perhaps you decided to ascend to the height of doing more than what you are paid to do. Have you ever looked around and not seen many people following you? Like the eagle, God did something awesome with you. God built in you God's own special respiratory system called the Holy Spirit. God enables you to fly at levels at which others cannot fly. Like the eagle, we can endeavor to seek those things that are above and experience God's best for our lives.

Now, you have the weapon. How are you going to use it?

Victory is mine! In the next 7 days, I will act on the following in order to Endeavor:

_____

_____

_____

_____

Chapter 14

Honor Those in Authority

"I grew up to always respect those in charge."
-Grant Hill

"... I myself am a man under authority, with soldiers under me."
-Matthew 8:9

Weapon #13: Honor Those in Authority

Why It Is Powerful

One of the greatest qualities of Joseph's character was the fact that he understood authority. He not only performed his tasks with excellence and enthusiasm, but also with respect and a great attitude. In our society, the notion of "being under authority" is one of the most misunderstood and abused principles. It is critical that we understand a vital key to success: **Authority is a system that was set up by God.** In fact, the first thing God did when God placed Adam and Eve in the Garden of Eden was to give them dominion or authority. To get a better understanding, let's look at what the Bible says in **Genesis 1:28.** It reads, **"And God blessed them, and God said unto them, be fruitful, and multiply (Mass Produce), and replenish the earth, and subdue it: and have dominion over the fish of the sea, and over the fowl of the air, and over every living thing that moves upon the earth."** Another translation for the word "dominion" is authority.

This system of authority that God instituted was a model of the same authority system that God established in heaven. The important thing to note here is that when Lucifer rebelled against God's authority, he was kicked out of heaven with the other rebellious angels. When we violate God's authority, we suffer the same consequences. Because God desires obedience and hates rebellion, He cannot bless us when we are not in a good place.

Strategy for Victory

Have you ever dealt with a difficult boss, who was unfair, unethical, or abusive? Did you get fed up and revert to backbiting, gossiping, or loafing, thinking that you were justified? Although you were the Christian, you engaged in bad behavior because you discovered that you got the short end of the stick while your boss seemed to be rewarded for their unjust deeds. Sound familiar? How many of us have experienced this scenario?

Perhaps the best biblical example of honoring those in authority is found in **Romans 13:1-8:**

> [1] **Let everyone be subject to the governing authorities, for there is no authority except that which God has established. The authorities that exist have been established by God.** [2] **Consequently, whoever rebels against the authority is rebelling against what God has instituted, and those who do so will bring judgment on themselves.** [3] **For rulers hold no terror for those who do right, but for those who do wrong. Do you want to be free from fear of the one in authority? Then do what is right and you will be commended.** [4] **For the one in authority is God's servant for your good. But if you do wrong, be afraid, for rulers do not bear the sword for no reason. They are God's servants, agents of wrath to bring punishment on the wrongdoer.** [5] **Therefore, it is necessary to submit to the authorities, not only because of possible punishment but also as a matter of conscience.**
>
> [6] **This is also why you pay taxes, for the authorities are God's servants, who give their full time to governing.** [7] **Give to everyone what you owe them: If you owe taxes, pay taxes; if revenue, then revenue; if respect, then respect; if honor, then honor.**

⁸ Let no debt remain outstanding, except the continuing debt to love one another, for whoever loves others has fulfilled the law.

Did you notice that there is no disclaimer in that passage? The scripture did not say "Be subject to higher powers, if they are nice to you," or "Be subject to higher powers, if they treat you fairly." Why do you think that is? Is God unfair? Does God "pick" on you? Absolutely not. He gives no disclaimer because God is concerned more about what we become, than what He can give us.

God is concerned about developing your character. You see, when our character is developed, then God can trust us. Joseph passed the character test. He had been treated unfairly more times than he could count. He was sold into slavery by his brothers and hated for his dream as a child. He was thrown into prison, only to serve years for a crime he did not commit. I mean if anyone had a right to complain or be bitter, it was Joseph. Yet, in all of scripture, there is not one place recorded where he ever complained about anything. Joseph passed one of the most difficult of all tests; he passed the test of operating properly under authority.

What was the result of Joseph's willingness to operate properly under authority? He was promoted and placed in authority, ultimately becoming the highest authority in the land, Prime Minster of Egypt. In fact, he was the most powerful man in the world at that time. Despite all of the setbacks Joseph faced, the line that always followed was this: "And the Lord was with Joseph, and caused him to prosper."

Let's contrast that with our society today. As a corporate trainer, I have interacted with hundreds of corporations and organizations. Unfortunately, it is not at all uncommon to hear, or even observe employees dishonor and disrespect their managers. How many times have you seen, heard, or partaken in dishonoring a manager or supervisor? I can certainly understand the frustration. No one likes to be treated unfairly or harshly. You may be asking, "What can I do to be productive when dealing with a difficult boss?" Keep reading.

Implementing the Strategy

7 Tactics to Honor Those in Authority on the Battlefield

1. **Find out what their communication style is and communicate with them accordingly.** Have you wondered why football teams

watch other teams' game films? They do it to understand their opponent's tendencies and strategies. What would happen were we to take this approach with our bosses. The possibilities would be limitless.

2. **Keep communication open.** Most of us never really learned how to communicate in our families. As a result, we have brought those same shortcomings into the workforce. If something doesn't go our way, it's either fight or flight. This is a poor strategy when it comes to working with our bosses. Take the initiative to let them know tactfully what is on your mind.

3. **Spend time developing your skills, rather than simply learning how to play the game. (Make this a priority)** One of the greatest ways to improve yourself and your relationship with your boss is to develop your skills.

4. **Don't depend on your boss to give you self esteem, depend on God. (Your identity is found only in God.)** You are who God says you are. Don't look to your boss for your self-worth. Understand that you are already approved by God.

5. **Be diligent and enthusiastic, rather than self-promoting (Let your work speak for itself.)** Joseph spent time doing three things: honoring God, doing a good job, and displaying a great attitude. Because of this, Joseph never had to spend time promoting himself. If we spend time in God's face, we don't have to spend time in other people's faces.

6. **Q.T.I.P. (Quit Taking It Personally)** Understand that everyone has a different style, and there are some people who will rub you the wrong way at times. It's alright to have emotions, but you should not be ruled by them. This tends to create difficulty in productivity and work relationships.

7. **Be Assertive and Proactive-give your boss feedback. (Don't just wait for things to happen, be a cause agent.)** John Madden said: "There are three types of people in this world, "Those who make things happen, those who watch things happen, and those who ask, 'What happened?'" Be a person who makes things happen.

For I am a man under authority, having soldiers under me: and I say to this man, Go, and he goeth; and to another, Come, and he cometh; and to my servant, Do this, and he doeth it. Matthew 8:9

Honoring those in authority builds character, and it is pleasing to God. We must not consider following the direction of our boss or other figures as a sign of weakness, but as a source of strength. We do so knowing that God has the ultimate authority. It is an authority that blesses us when we follow God's direction for our lives. The same applies in our careers. When we excel at our work, we receive blessings and just rewards in due season... we can, indeed, rise from the pit to the palace.

Now, you have the weapon. How are you going to use it?

Victory is mine! In the next 7 days, I will act on the following in order to Honor Authority:

_____

_____

_____

_____

Chapter 15

Crucify Excuses

"Excuses are nails used to build houses of failure."
-Creflo A. Dollar

"But they all alike began to make excuses."
Luke 14:18

Weapon #14: Crucify Excuses

Why It Is Powerful

One of the most important moves we must make, if we are to be truly productive is to crucify excuses. Have you ever stopped to consider the wonder of the cross? Because of Calvary, Jesus came and took away many things. He took away our sin. He took away our shame. However, what we often overlook is that by taking away our sin and shame Jesus took away our excuses.

Since the fall of Adam, humankind has been making excuses. If the day and age in which we live is characterized by anything, it is excuses. Soon after Eve first sinned by taking the fruit as Adam stood by, another shameful first took place: the world's first excuse. God, in His holiness, asked Adam a question that has altered humankind's destiny: **"Have you eaten from the tree that I commanded you not to** eat from?" **(Genesis 3:11)** What was Adam's answer? **"The woman you put here with me—she gave me some fruit from the tree, and I ate it." (Genesis 3:12)** Since then, excuses have been coming forth as often as inhaling and exhaling.

The interesting thing about Adam's excuse was that he not only blamed Eve, but he also blamed God in the process. The same God who had shown him amazing love and had given him dominion over everything was now the scapegoat for his own failure. Let's listen to the words again, to get a better understanding: "The woman you put here with me—she gave me some fruit from the tree, and I ate it." In other words, "If you hadn't given her to me, I wouldn't have sinned." This same saga continues today.

The Power of The Cross

When Jesus came and redeemed humankind at Calvary, He forever set the high water mark for suffering. Have you ever wondered why God chose, of all things, the crucifixion as Jesus' method of death? Why didn't God have him beheaded, like the Apostle Paul, or some other easier form of execution? The reason, I believe, was that the crucifixion was the most agonizing form of death known to that society at the time. In fact, men would sometimes hang on the cross for days before dying.

God loved us so much, that it says in the book of Isaiah, **"but it pleased the Lord to bruise Him." (Isaiah 53:10)** The cross became something great. It became an eternal reference point for suffering and excuse elimination. God did this so that no matter what challenge we were facing in life, the question could be asked: "Have you ever suffered as Christ did?" When facing challenges as Christians, we still sometimes think that we're the only ones in the world who are going through tough times. We think no one could possibly identify with our unique trial, persecution, or challenge. The Bible says otherwise. In fact, the Word tells us that **"Jesus was in all points tempted like unto man, but without sin." (Hebrews 4:15)** That meant that Jesus had faced and conquered every form of temptation that human beings have faced, including the one you didn't, the cross. The cross is a constant reminder that we can endure more than we think is possible, love more than we think is reasonable, and maximize our potential to achieve the impossible. In other words, there is no room for excuses.

Strategy for Victory

Action 1: Avoid The "Minority" Trap

One of the most rampant spirits that has plagued humankind for ages is the spirit of racism. It has been alive since biblical times, and Satan has used it to attack and discourage God's people for ages. Although racism exists in our society, sometimes victims of racism fall prey to using chronic, unjust treatment as an excuse for failure. In this regard, the victim is doubly defeated because of historical oppression and because the "minority" trap can be used as an escape from the demands of God's calling. One of the things that history tells us about minorities is that people whom society has labeled as such usually have endured some type of great suffering. However, most of the people that God used in the Bible were minorities in the societies in which they lived.   Take a look at the Minority Hall of Fame.

The Minority Hall of Fame

- Daniel

- Nehemiah

- Joseph

- Esther

- Moses

The problem with the habit of using one's minority status as an excuse is that people don't realize that they are insulting God. By magnifying their perceived problem, they are de-magnifying the Lord. The Bible says that we are to "magnify" the Lord. The word "magnify" literally means "to make large." By spending so much time talking about being a minority, we are saying to God that He is not able to handle the injustice of racism in our lives.

Action 2: Avoid Declaring: "Everybody Keeps Walkin' Over Me"

Another common excuse to justify a lack of production is: "Everybody keeps walking over me!" How many times have you heard people complain about not being able to perform because someone is always walking over them? It could be an unfair boss, or perhaps a coworker acting without integrity. It could be a customer or client who is a constant source of frustration. It could be anyone who seems to take our power away from us without regard. If there is one thing that characterizes this age more than anything else it is the tendency to blame others. Blame should be characterized as the cancer of the twenty-first century. Few things zap a person's productivity as much as blame. Blame is destructive for two reasons. First, it is a tool designed by Satan to destroy us. Second, it causes one to justify bad performance – automatically.

I understand that people get "walked over," particularly as Christians. Warfare comes in all forms, especially in the work environment. Why is this? I believe it is in the workplace that we earn money to give back to God. It is here that we are either preparing for or living out our life's calling; it is also the place where we tend to spend the majority of our time.

Just because we experience warfare, does not mean that we can't perform and overcome. **Philippians 4:13** says, **"I can do all things through Christ who strengthens me."** If anyone understood being "walked over" it was Jesus. He was rejected by the Pharisees, called illegitimate, and labeled a fraud. Yet every time He was called upon, He produced results, whether it was by healing the sick, casting out devils, or saving humanity. Let's examine what Jesus said in **Matthew 5:13** about being "walked over," where he said, **"You are the salt of the earth. But if the salt loses its saltiness, how can it be made salty again? It is no longer good for anything, except to be thrown out and trampled underfoot."**

If you've been trampled under the feet of men and women, I have a very important question to ask you. Have you lost your savor? Have you lost your enthusiasm, zest, and zeal? By Jesus' own words this is what causes us to be "walked over." If anybody needs to be enthusiastic and zealous for excellence, it ought to be God's people. Note what the Word tells us about King David's zeal and enthusiasm. **Psalm 69:9** says, **"For zeal for your house consumes me..."** Because of his zeal, King David was known as the mighty conqueror and not the mightily conquered. Likewise, when our zeal and enthusiasm are fresh, we shall be mighty conquerors.

Furthermore, consider the passion and zeal of Jesus. While praying in the Garden of Gethsemane, he sweated drops of blood.

Jesus knew he would be crucified. He saw the agony that He would face. Still, we were His passion despite His human pain. If anybody has a reason to be thankful and joyful, it should be us.

Action 3: Avoid Complaining: "Nobody Ever Notices My Performance"

I have had the pleasure of traveling extensively throughout North America to provide training for managers and staff members at a variety of corporations. During my travels, one of the biggest complaints I receive from employees is that their managers never recognize them for their performance. It might surprise you to know this, but most managers and supervisors consistently fail to even to thank their employees for a job well done. What's worse is that over the years surveys have shown that recognition from management has consistently ranked as the number one motivator for employees.

Without question, any good manager should absolutely praise employees for doing a good job. However, the question is this: What happens when they don't? Have you ever known people to fail to do something that they should do? I know you're thinking, "Only every day!" In fact, I have found that more times than not managers fail to do what they should. Does this justify the employee failing to give their best? A thousand times "No."

To better answer the question, let's examine what Jesus had to say about the subject. In **Matthew 5:14-16** he said, **"You are the light of the world. A town built on a hill cannot be hidden. Neither do people light a lamp and put it under a bowl. Instead they put it on its stand, and it gives light to everyone in the house.** In the same way, let your light shine before others, that they may see your good deeds and glorify your Father in heaven. Have you hidden your light under a bowl, where no one can see it? Or have you truly put it on a stand or a candlestick, displaying excellence at its finest, despite the opposition? Here, Jesus silences all arguments, and answers all questions with His first statement. **"A town built upon a hill cannot be hidden."** The fact that Jesus said it automatically makes it the truth. When we truly let our light so shine before people, they will see our good works and glorify our Father in heaven. Let your light shine.

Implementing the Strategy

7 Tactics to Crucify Excuses on the Battlefield

1. **Under promise, and over deliver.** No matter how small the promise, honor it. If you cannot do it, do not promise it. It is better to make no promise and keep it, than make a promise and break it.

2. **Accept responsibility for the problems you create - immediately.** Determine to eliminate blame totally from your person. You will have to bite your tongue sometimes, but an expanding of the spirit will take place inside of you. You will begin to change from the inside out. Eventually others will see it, too.

3. **Learn to say "no."** In order for us to be true to ourselves and to God, we must be delivered from the bondage of people. Ensure that your motives are pure. Saying no does not make you a bad person.

4. **Prepare better.** One of the biggest reasons that people break commitments is bad planning. How many times have you been late because you didn't give yourself enough time? Determine to start early, and give yourself plenty of time. You'll be amazed at your productivity.

5. **Acknowledge accountability.** Get friends to hold you accountable for keeping your commitments. Make sure you choose a friend that will be honest with you and who cares about your development.

6. **Write down your goals and review them daily.** Start your day fresh with a plan. Start small with a to-do list. Cross off tasks as you complete them. Your confidence level will increase, and it will become contagious.

7. **Read your Bible, particularly the books of Proverbs and Ecclesiastes.** Ask God for wisdom. Be confident that God hears, and answers. Read yourself into the Word. Understand that the Word is simply a chronicle of God doing extraordinary things with ordinary people. Why not you?

Because of the power of the cross, you can crucify excuses. The brutality of Jesus' crucifixion and Jesus' ultimate sacrifice for the salvation of humankind vetoes any excuse we can make.

Now, you have the weapon. How are you going to use it?

Victory is mine! In the next 7 days, I will act on the following in order to Crucify Excuses:

_____

_____

_____

_____

Chapter 16

Bounce Higher

"Success is never final, failure is never fatal,
it is courage that counts."

-Sir Winston Churchill

"Brothers and sisters, I do not consider myself yet
to have taken hold of it. But one thing I do:
Forgetting what is behind and straining toward what is ahead,"

-Philippians 3:13

Weapon #15: Bounce Higher

Why It Is Powerful

In order for us to be Mass Producers, it is imperative that when we fall we bounce back higher than before we fell. We must begin again with a fresh and new start. So often we hear the phrases "bouncing back from defeat," and "bouncing back from failure." They are reminders that we must be resilient, durable, and tough, in order to be successful. It is absolutely vital that we bounce back from failure and defeat. However, it is equally as important to bounce higher. In other words, we must learn from our mistakes.

When I was growing up, we had these amazing little balls called "Superballs." I would carry them in my pocket everywhere I went.

My friends and I would have bouncing contests to see whose ball could bounce the highest. These little balls seemed as though they could bounce into eternity. They would bounce so high we would sometimes lose sight of them in the air. What great fun we would have as we tried with all of our might to out bounce one another. Whenever someone bounced their ball higher than mine, I would proclaim, "You wait until next time! Next time is gonna be different." God created us in similar fashion to those balls, in two aspects. First, we were created to bounce high. Second, even when we face failure, we should still be confident in our future success.

Can you recall the last time you looked out of the window of a skyscraper, or the window of a plane, or looked out from any high place? If you're like me you probably experienced a feeling of grandeur, freedom, and power. That's because God designed you that way. You were created to have dominion over the earth. When you are taking in the scene from a high altitude, that experience is very similar to what it means to seek those things above mere earthly limits. It means we are to seek the higher things in life, or to see those things which are above, where Christ sits.

Our understanding of this truth gives new meaning to what Paul says in **Philippians 4:8** when he says, **"Finally, brothers and sisters, whatever is true, whatever is noble, whatever is right, whatever is pure, whatever is lovely, whatever is admirable—if anything is excellent or praiseworthy—think about such things."** After the Fall, God made the serpent crawl on his belly, and that is his domain. Our adversary, Satan, was relegated by God to the ground. The only way that he can touch us is if we lower ourselves to his level. As long as we are seeking the high and holy things of God, Satan has no dominion over us.

Strategy for Victory

God has built into our character a holy durability, elasticity, and ability to come back from defeat. What was it that made the Superball bounce so high? It was throwing it down harder, which brings us to a great truth for those who are truly committed to Christ: **The harder the fall, the higher the bounce!** You are tougher than you think you are, and you will not break as easily as you think. **Proverbs 24:16** states, **"For though the righteous fall seven times, they rise again..."** In this scripture are three truths to help you declare the victory.

Truth #1: Everyone, no matter how good they are can fall.

For though the righteous fall...

Wow! You mean good and righteous people fall, too? Yep! Though many believe that people who seem to have it all together, or who seem to be devout Christians never fall or stumble, the Word is clear that none of us is without sin. It even goes on to say that if we say we have no sin, we lie. You see, unfortunately, when Adam fell in the Garden, one of the things we inherited was his sinful nature. As a result, we will be tempted by sin, and we will occasionally fall. However, the beautiful thing about the power of the cross is that since Jesus redeemed humankind, we can now be victorious over sin and its power. We no longer are enslaved in sin and its dominion, but rather we now have dominion over it. Hallelujah!

Truth #2: You will fall more than once.

...seven times...

The writer of Proverbs lets us know that falling is something we have to battle as human beings. Furthermore, it suggests that we are going to have to fight the good fight of faith, if we are to be victorious. Seven times lets us know that the challenges of life are constant and certain – no matter who you are. The term "seven" here indicates a period of time, or a process. This is not something that just happens every now and then. Over time we will need to exercise total dependence on God's power, grace, and love. Thank God we have Jesus and the Holy Spirit to equip and empower us to be victorious. The Apostle Paul writes about his struggles with sin in **Romans 7:24: "What a wretched man I am! Who will rescue me from this body that is subject to death?"** How many of us have cried out like Paul? I know I have! The next line is the one that shoots us into spiritual orbit. It reads: "Thanks be to God, who delivers me through Jesus Christ our Lord!" Thank God for Jesus!

Truth #3: You will rise from the fall.

...they rise again.

What makes us rise again? I mean surely, it would have to get pretty frustrating to keep falling. Yet, as surely as we must fall, we must rise. The powerfully important thing that makes us rise is what we know. We rise when we focus on the righteousness in Christ Jesus and our understanding of who we are in God. This knowledge gives us the spiritual yeast to rise. So as we suffer through the bruises that can come with a fall, we must understand that our righteousness or justification was not earned, but given by God's grace. It is that grace that lifts us to our feet to continue the journey. What a great gift the grace of God is.

The Power of Repentance

One of the greatest gifts that God gave us as believers is the gift of repentance. When Jesus died for our sins on Calvary, a great exchange took place – Jesus' righteousness for our sin. Now that's what I call a deal! We did nothing to earn it, and He said that we have been "made righteous by the blood of Jesus." The Bible says in Romans that we have been "made righteous." That meant that we did nothing to earn it, but we received it because Jesus took our sin for His righteousness. God even calls us righteous. The only thing we had to do was receive God's righteousness as a free gift. It is this great truth that causes us to rise, and to throw off any cloaks of condemnation, inadequacy, or fear. When we know who we are and whose we are, we cannot be held down or defeated ever again.

So what about the unrighteous or the unjust?

In order for us to fully understand what makes the righteous or just person rise, we must ask, "So, what about the unrighteous or unjust?" This is certainly a great question. How many people do you know who have great strengths and qualities as people? I happen to know many non-Christians who possess better character than some of my friends who are Christians. Yet, they seem to stay down and defeated. Why don't they rise? What is the source of the weight they carry?

They don't possess that great truth and liberty of being "made righteous." They have allowed guilt, shame, condemnation, and all kinds of other ills from Satan to beat them up. They are carrying a burden that God never intended for them to have to carry. Jesus speaks about these burdens when He extends to us this great appeal: **"Come to me, all you who are weary and burdened, and I will give you rest. Take my yoke upon you and learn from me, for I am gentle and humble in heart, and you will find rest for your souls. For my yoke is easy and my burden is light." (Matthew 11:28-30)** It is great to know that when we come to Christ, we no longer have to carry that burden of sin. Because of Jesus, we can now "stand fast therefore in the great liberty in which Christ has made us free." Praise God.

If you feel as if you have fallen seven times, and plenty more, let me commend you for having the courage to rise again. Let me commend you for having the courage to get up one more time after being knocked down. There is power in the cross. There is power in what was accomplished on Calvary to encourage all of us on this journey called life.

Your decision to read this book is evidence of your desire to live like Jesus and to be your best for Him. I would like to share with you a great truth that should be celebrated daily. **There is power in your rising!** A great thing happens when you rise again. When you rise again, you are acting most like Jesus because after the third day, He rose again. He didn't stay in the grave, but he rose! Hallelujah! There is power in your rising! You see God knew that you would stumble and fall. So, when He created you, He built into your makeup a success mechanism called the Holy Spirit. God breathed into you as a believer his life, the very life of God. This blessing gives us the ability to rise out of every situation we face.

Implementing the Strategy

7 Reflective Questions to Bounce Higher on the Battlefield

1. What destructive habits do I find myself repeating continually? Determine to break them and deny them access to your life.

2. What valuable lesson have I learned from my last failure? Determine not to continue to repeat the same mistakes again.

3. How is this failure connected to my calling in life? Is this some problem that God is using me to solve for humanity? Determine to follow His direction.

4. Determine what inspirational source was helpful in your bouncing higher. Use it to bounce higher in the future.

5. What books can I read, people I can speak with, or websites I can visit to enable me to bounce higher the next time? Make a decision to act on your answers immediately.

6. Is my imbalanced living hurting my ability to succeed? For example, will getting back into proper fitness and nutrition help me in other areas of my life? Do I need to spend more quality time with my family? Whatever your challenges are, deal with them. Sometimes the greatest progress happens in a not so obvious manner.

7. Have I allowed this failure to affect my self-esteem or confidence? Have I allowed the enemy to use guilt and condemnation against me? Perhaps this is the time to spend time building yourself up by confessing God's word over your life. Maybe this is the time intensify your fellowship with covenant friends and church attendance. Make a decision to act on it.

An interesting thing happened after Jesus was born that speaks directly to what I am saying about the power of our ability to rise. In the book of Luke, Mary and Joseph bring baby Jesus to the temple to dedicate him to God. They are greeted by a Godly older man by the name of Simeon, who has been waiting to see the Messiah face to face. Upon holding Jesus, Simeon begins to prophesy to Mary, and he says something very powerful that speaks to all of us. He says, "This child is set for the fall and rising again of many." Glory! Isn't it interesting and great that he didn't say the rise and fall. Why did he say this? Perhaps it was because he knew that the power was in the rising again. Amen!

Now, you have the weapon. How are you going to use it?

Victory is mine! In the next 7 days, I will act on the following in order to Bounce Higher:

_____

_____

_____

_____

Chapter 17

Make Necessary Adjustments

"We cannot direct the wind, but we can adjust the sails."

"Do not conform to the pattern of this world, but be transformed by the renewing of your mind."

Weapon #16: Make Necessary Adjustments

Why It Is Powerful

Making adjustments puts us on the path to God's destiny for our lives. Sometimes, we bite off more than we can chew when setting goals for change. We try unsuccessfully to make 50%, 60%, and 70% improvements, only to come up short. Many times, only small adjustments can catapult us into where we want to be.

A great example of this concept was the 2010 Super Bowl. The Indianapolis Colts were playing the New Orleans Saints. The Colts, a superior team on paper, and led by MVP Peyton Manning, jumped out to an early lead. The first half of the game ended with the Colts holding a comfortable lead, and it appeared that they were headed to an easy win. Nevertheless, the Saints were coached by the quick-thinking and unorthodox Sean Peyton. As the second half began, an interesting thing happened. The Saints opened with an onside kick, normally used as a last resort in the closing minutes of a game. The startled and unsuspecting Colts lineman fumbled the football, and the Saints recovered. An eager Saints offense, led by Drew Brees, quickly scored, and the entire momentum of the game shifted. The Saints would go on to win their first Super Bowl in franchise history all because of one key play. This one important adjustment was responsible for changing the entire mood of the game, inspiring a team and a city to victory. It could well be said that this adjustment was responsible for giving a hurting city something great to believe in again.

Subsequently, when we make necessary adjustments, we, too, can capitalize by changing the momentum of our lives. One of the things I love best about our great and awesome God is that God never changes His character, but we must be sensitive to God's shifts in circumstances. We cannot put God in a box. As God shifts into another gear, we must shift with Him or be left behind, missing significant opportunities in life. **Ecclesiastes 3 says, "There is a time for everything, and a season for every activity under the heavens."** This means that we must be alert and sensitive to the Holy Spirit. When the seasons change we must likewise make adjustments and adapt to the Holy Spirit.

Strategy for Victory

I am probably the world's biggest boxing fan. In fact, were you to look up "boxing fan" in Webster's dictionary, there would probably be a picture of me smiling! My father, a New York Golden Gloves Champion, use to let me watch old black-and-white films of Joe Louis and Sugar Ray Robinson. I know that many consider boxing to be a brutal sport, but I like it because of the tactical prowess that it takes to be a champion. In order to become a champion, a fighter must be willing and able to make necessary adjustments.

For example, if you are fighting a left-handed boxer, you may have to adjust your stance. You may have to develop your ability to punch with a hand with which you typically do not use. If you are facing a fighter who is bigger or stronger, you may have to rely more on your hand speed, quickness, and smarts to beat him to the punch. If your opponent is strong, but short-winded, you may have to make them miss, cover up, and allow them to run out of gas by punching themselves out. Whatever is necessary, the champion must make the necessary adjustments. Some adjustments are large, and some are small, but you must make adjustments if you plan to win.

Another way to imagine the skill of "making adjustments" is to consider the effort of an airline pilot. Most people are unaware of how many times a pilot must make adjustments to arrive safely at a destination. In essence, they are adjusting their course throughout the flight, and are constantly making necessary adjustments to follow the flight plan. Yet, how often have you, as a passenger, arrived at an unanticipated destination? We usually arrive safely at our destinations. Like the pilot of the aircraft, we must make adjustments as we pilot our own lives. At the same time, we must always remember that God is our air traffic controller. When we follow His lead and make the necessary adjustments, we will arrive safely at our destination called SUCCESS.

Implementing the Strategy

7 Reflective Questions to Make Necessary Adjustments on the Battlefield

1. What one important adjustment can you make that would be easier than expected? Make it at once.

2. What one adjustment have you simply put off because of procrastination or fear? Attack it, and act on it immediately.

3. What one change could you make that would totally revolutionize your life? Face it, and act on it.

4. What one habit could you break that would cause you to rise immediately? Take steps to act on it now.

5. What one negative person should you make the adjustment to not hang around? Do it now!

6. What one significant change would be the most difficult to make that would yield the greatest return? Determine to act on it first.

7. What negative atmosphere is stifling your creativity and progress? Determine to leave it immediately if at all possible, and certainly as soon as possible.

The key to making necessary adjustments is to recognize the need as early as possible and effectively shift your actions, thoughts, or plans. Then, trust that God will create the path for you to follow.

Now, you have the weapon. How are you going to use it?

Victory is mine! In the next 7 days, I will act on the following in order to Make Necessary Adjustments:

_____

_____

_____

_____

Chapter 18

Play With Pain

Tough times never last, but tough people do."
-Dr. Robert Schuler

"Join with me in suffering, like a good soldier of Christ Jesus."
II Timothy 2:3

Weapon #17: Play With Pain

Why It Is Powerful

Playing with pain is a harsh reality to accept, but it separates winners from losers. By playing with pain, I mean that players continue to perform well, despite their challenges with pain. I would like to clarify here that I am not emphasizing emotional rather than physical pain. There are many types of emotional pain that can affect our attitudes and ability to be productive. Some pains are disappointments from the past. Some are mistreatments by employers, loved ones, or the like. Some hurts may be the economic conditions under which one is living currently. Let me pause here and acknowledge that we live in a hurting world. I understand that many people are dealing with tremendous pains on multiple levels. I have learned that pain will come in life, and that we are not always prepared for its consequences. Pain and suffering affect our outlook, and sometimes cause us to question the eternal presence of God.

However, it is important that we do not use our hurts as an excuse for bad behavior or bad performance. Do you recall marveling at someone else who seemed to perform at their best, even as they were hurting, physically, emotionally, or spiritually? Did you notice that they maintained a great attitude at the same time? Maybe someone marveled at you. When we play with pain, we reinforce our commitment to whatever it is that we are on a mission to accomplish. Our steadfast commitment propels us to achievement, regardless of the difficulty we may be experiencing.

Strategy for Victory

We can't always determine the way we feel. The one thing **that we have** complete control over is our attitude. To quote **Eleanor Roosevelt**, "No one can make you feel inferior without your **consent."** To that end, we cannot wallow in our pain unless we give it permission to engulf us. Ultimately, we still have jobs to do and people to serve, so our commitment to the cause at hand overrides any pain. Our attitude must reflect commitment.

Our challenge is that many of us sincerely believe that we possess a true commitment to our life's work. But do we? Perhaps you know someone who is committed by his or her own standards. Maybe no one ever tells them the truth, either desiring to be polite or fearing the outcome of telling the truth. However, there is a three word question that would greatly assist them in their analysis: "Compared to what?" Without having a comparison or gauge, how can one truly measure their commitment? What is lacking is the very thing that would be beneficial – commitment. Unless we are big enough to accept credible observations regarding our performance, we cannot say that we are truly committed. Commitment without critique is not really commitment at all. It robs us of our character development, and robs our employers and clients of our best service.

According to world renowned speaker and philanthropist, Peter J. Daniels, "Commitment is the willingness to bear pain as a necessary cost toward the benefit." There are certain costs that are involved with achieving anything in life. Whenever we say that we desire to have something, the proof will be evidenced by the price that we are willing to pay to achieve it. One of the best examples of this is found in **II Timothy 2:3-4**. Paul writes to his spiritual son, Timothy about being strong. He says, **"Join with me in suffering, like a good soldier**

of Christ Jesus. No one serving as a soldier gets entangled in civilian affairs, but rather tries to please his commanding officer."

Today, very few people understand the importance of playing with pain. Lost in their difficult circumstances, they tend to act as if no one else has experienced pain except them. Nothing could be farther from the truth. There are countless others who have endured incomprehensible hardships and do so with a positive attitude. Still, many believe that their pain justifies bad behavior. Subsequently, they short circuit their careers, as well as their progress by allowing their emotions to disrupt their advancement.

Daily, we encounter people coping with pain, but not playing with pain. Think about it. How many times have you been in conversation with someone who spends all of their time talking about some wrong that has been done to them? Perhaps you interact with someone working in some capacity of customer service. A casual conversation turns into an earful about the shortcomings of their job, the recent bad weather, and the problems of the country. It is as if they have forgotten that you were there waiting to be served. Now let me say here that I certainly can appreciate and understand that people experience hurt and wrong. I have certainly experienced my share. However, we tend to magnify what we choose to focus on. What would happen if we gave as much attention to the flawless execution of our duties, as we did the wrong done against us? The possibilities would be limitless. Furthermore, so often, we talk to people who can tell us not only who wronged them, but every detail regarding their troubles. They have become so acquainted with their bad experience that they camp out there, forgetting to keep living. These people are coping with their pain, not playing with their pain. Are you coping or playing?

Implementing the Strategy

7 Reflective Questions to Play With Pain on the Battlefield

1. In what area have I complained where I know deep down that I have not done my best? Take action and attack it immediately.

2. What friends or colleagues hold me accountable and inspire courage, action, and toughness in me? Welcome their feedback and act on it.

3. What good habit have I stopped that was painful, but inspired toughness in me? Resurrect it, and act on it again.

4. What person in my life inspires me to be my best and to do my best? Engage their feedback.

5. What inspirational music, story, or resource could I draw strength from to inspire me to play better with pain? Engage it immediately.

6. What inspirational person who has played with pain could you draw strength from? Use their story to inspire you to action.

7. Would my playing with pain inspire someone I know to do the same? Who might that person be? Use that as a motivating factor.

In order to play with pain, we must acknowledge the pain and **keep going.** It can be paralyzing, but commitment will free us to grasp **our greatest** victory.

Now, you have the weapon. How are you going to use it?

Victory is mine! In the next 7 days, I will act on the following in order to Play With Pain successfully:

_____

_____

_____

_____

Chapter 19

Do The Impossible

"It always seems impossible until it's done."
-Nelson Mandela

"For with God, nothing shall be impossible."
-Luke 1:37 (KJV)

Weapon #18: Do the Impossible

Why It Is Powerful

We were created on this planet to serve God by being productive. We were not created to strike a pose, or simply exist, but to bear fruit. One of the reasons Jesus cursed the fig tree was because it wasn't producing fruit. Even though it had lush, beautiful leaves, it had no figs on it. The Lord himself said, "Every tree that does not bear fruit is cut down." I always wondered why Jesus cursed the fig tree. At first I thought, hey, maybe it was just a bad tree. How many times have you picked up a bad apple or a bad orange? Maybe it was just a bad tree.

It wasn't until I read the passage several times that I noticed one of the most important lines in the passage. The book actually reads, "It wasn't the season for figs." How in the world could Jesus expect the fig tree to produce when it was out of season? Then, suddenly it hit me like a ton of bricks! When the Lord of creation asks you for some figs, you had better give Him some! You see Jesus is Lord of all. He created everything and owned everything, including you. Because He created the fig tree, He knew what the fig tree was capable of doing. It would be illogical for God to expect something from you that you couldn't possibly produce.

Many of us are no different from the fig tree. God keeps asking us to produce fruit, and yet all we can produce are excuses. We complain that the conditions or seasons are not in the right order to produce. We either come up short or not at all. Isn't it great that God blesses us 365 days a year?

What's worse is we even tell God what's impossible. Imagine that! We don't just tell God what we can't do, but we tell God what He can't do either. The only thing that can be deemed impossible is something that cannot be achieved by God. Everything else falls within the realm of possibility. A very respectable organization once gave Napoleon Hill, author of the classic book, *Think and Grow Rich*, a dictionary as a gift. Mr. Hill thanked the organization for offering the gift; however, he refused to accept it. Why did he refuse? The dictionary contained the word "impossible." He said he could accept the gift only if the page containing the word impossible was left out. The man presenting the gift promptly tore out the page, and Mr. Hill gladly accepted the gift.

2 Things That Are Impossible With God

> **Lying**
>
> **Failure**

Strategy for Victory

The Gospel of Matthew gives us an account of the importance of productivity, and its benefits and eventual blessings. More important, in this popular story of the talents, we receive a lesson on what can happen when we do not take risks. Risk taking is critical for us to do the impossible. **Matthew 25:14-25** gives an account of a man traveling to a far country. Before he leaves, he delivers his goods to his servants or managers.

It reads as follows:

¹⁴For the kingdom of heaven is as a man travelling into a far country, who called his own servants, and delivered unto them his goods.

[15]And unto one he gave five talents, to another two, and to another one; to every man according to his several ability; and straightway took his journey.

[16]Then he that had received the five talents went and traded with the same, and made them other five talents.

[17]And likewise he that had received two, he also gained other two.

[18]But he that had received one went and digged in the earth, and hid his lord's money.

[19]After a long time the lord of those servants cometh, and reckoned with them.

[20]And so he that had received five talents came and brought other five talents, saying, Lord, thou delivered unto me five talents: behold, I have gained beside them five talents more.

[21]His lord said unto him, Well done, thou good and faithful servant: thou hast been faithful over a few things, I will make thee ruler over many things: enter thou into the joy of thy lord.

[22]He also that had received two talents came and said, Lord, thou delivered unto me two talents: behold, I have gained two other talents beside them.

[23]His lord said unto him, Well done, good and faithful servant; thou hast been faithful over a few things, I will make thee ruler over many things: enter thou into the joy of thy lord.

[24]Then he which had received the one talent came and said, Lord, I knew thee that thou art an hard man, reaping where thou hast not sown, and gathering where thou hast not strawed:

[25]And I was afraid, and went and hid thy talent in the earth: lo, there thou hast that is thine.

[26]His lord answered and said unto him, Thou wicked and slothful servant, thou knewest that I reap where I sowed not, and gather where I have not strawed:

[27]Thou oughtest therefore to have put my money to the exchangers, and then at my coming I should have received mine own with usury.

²⁸**Take therefore the talent from him, and give it unto him which hath ten talents.**

²⁹**For unto every one that hath shall be given, and he shall have abundance: but from him that hath not shall be taken away even that which he hath.**

³⁰**And cast ye the unprofitable servant into outer darkness: there shall be weeping and gnashing of teeth.**

Let's take a closer look at the unprofitable servant in order to learn from his mistakes. First, all of the servants were given money according to their individual abilities. The master knew the capability of the unprofitable servant, so he only gave the servant what he could handle. He didn't necessarily expect him to produce more than the other servants. He only wanted for him to do his best. Like this servant, the problem with most people is that they don't even try. They do not take the risk.

Second, the master wanted the servants to think for themselves. How many problems could be solved if we would simply take time to think? The servant in this scripture was not only lazy, but he had a lazy, slothful mind. As believers we should keep our minds and attitudes fresh and free of things like gossip, murmuring, and complaining. These only lead to non-productive tendencies.

Finally, the servant said he was afraid. I don't want criticize him for being afraid. We are all afraid at times. Anyone who claims that he or she has never been afraid a time or two is probably being dishonest. It was not the fear, itself, that was problematic, but what the fear caused the servant to do. He hid his talent, rendering it non-productive.

Like so many people today, the last servant thought fear justified his lack of productivity. As Christians, it is important that we take inventory of our lives and realize that we have everything we need to be successful. II Peter 1:3 says it best when it states that God's power "has given us everything we need for a godly life through our knowledge of him who called us by his own glory and goodness." God has preordained your success. He has already made allowances for your failures, and understands your weakness and limitations. What God wants you to realize is this great truth: It is not based on your ability or power anyway! God is not asking you to do the impossible in your own power, because you'd fail every time. Why do you suppose in **John 15:5**, Jesus said, **"Apart from me you can do nothing."**? It was because God knew that He is the source of our power. Have you ever experienced a shortage of power, due to a blown outlet? That's what it's like when you try to rely on your own strength in doing the impossible. You will always come up short. When you plug your power cord into God's outlet, the power is unlimited!

Implementing the Strategy

7 Tactics to Do the Impossible on the Battlefield

1. **Examine an area of your life where you have made excuses.** Determine to overcome that area of your life. Ask yourself the question, "What tangible steps must I take to make this happen?"

2. **Read and apply the word of God to your life.** There is power in the word! Ask yourself the question: In what ways have I allowed fear to paralyze my productivity? The word will infuse the faith needed to inspire you to act. Act in faith. Remember, without faith, it is impossible to please God.

3. **Confess the word of God over your life.** Determine what you want to achieve, and then write down the corresponding scriptures that support them. Confess them as affirmations over your life daily and see God's power work in your life. Remember, life and death are in the power of the tongue.

4. **Begin to think outside of the box.** Change your paradigm concerning what is impossible. Remember what Jesus said. "With man it is impossible, but with God all things are possible." Remember, things that are now possible were once impossibilities.

5. **Practice.** Determine to become better at what you do. Gather vital information on the subject that you want to improve on. Speak with people who are experts in the field that you wish to improve in and ask them to mentor you. Some of the greatest performers of all times have been understudies of the great.

6. **Focus on your goal of becoming excellent**—eliminate distractions to your excellent performance. Unfortunately, this will include unnecessary time-wasters, such as negative people and situations that distract you.

7. **Seek out the right team of associates and people to assist you in becoming excellent.** Don't try to do it all on your own. Synergize! Work smarter, not harder. Some goals will only be achieved by cooperating with others.

Now, you have the weapon. How are you going to use it?

Victory is mine! In the next 7 days, I will act on the following in order to Do the Impossible:

_____

_____

_____

_____

Chapter 20

Seize The Day!

"Well done is better than well said."
- Benjamin Franklin

"Faith without works is dead."
James 2:20

Weapon #19: Seize the Day!

Why It Is Powerful

"Carpe diem!" We can use these words by the Roman poet, Horace, as a rallying cry in the battle to become mass producers. Seize the day! That is what Horace meant. If we follow the poet's command, we can begin to understand the power and possibility that one day possesses. Then, we can commit to seize that same power and possibility to meet the purpose in our lives. **Psalm 118:24** says, **"This is the day that the Lord has made, we will rejoice and be glad in it."** This poignant scripture means that this is a day in which anything is possible. It is another day that God has allowed us to see because of God's grace and mercy. It is another twenty-four hours of life which God has given us to fulfill His plan and mission in our lives.

Strategy for Victory

Action 1: Ask For Forgiveness

One of the greatest things about being a Christian, and something too often taken for granted, is that no matter what you've done, if you ask God for forgiveness you are **immediately** forgiven! It is easy to allow past mistakes to haunt you. However, in order to seize the day and the blessings God has for you, you must welcome forgiveness so you can thrive. To quote my friend and motivational speaker, Jimmie Lucas: "Yesterday ended at midnight!"

Action 2: Use Your Time Wisely

This may be a hard question: How much time do you waste on worthless pursuits that lead to nothing? Mass producers utilize their time wisely. They value their time, as well as the time of others. They are keen and alert to opportunities, knowing that those windows may soon close, never to come again. If you ever feel as if you have wasted your time and your days, remind yourself of two important things.

1. God holds all of us responsible and accountable for what God has called us to do.

2. There are endless possibilities of what can happen in only one day.

Seize the Day!: A Few Examples

In one day, God through Moses, delivered 2 million Jews from Egyptian captivity, and they came out with all of the wealth.

In one day, God slew 185,000 Assyrians, without a single fight, through King Hezekiah.

In one day, on July 3, 1863, Colonel Joshua Chamberlain at Gettysburg with only 80 men and no ammunition captured over 400 Rebel soldiers. That battle was said to have won the civil war.

In one day, over 1 million African Americans led by Dr. Martin Luther King, Jr., marched on Washington, DC. Dr. King proceeded to deliver his famous, "I Have A Dream" speech. This speech captured the hearts and conscience of Americans of all races and creeds. It is said that this was the day Black America truly became free.

In one day, Joan of Arc infused courage into her nation to resist the domination by the England over France

In one day, on a hill called Calvary, God redeemed humankind by sending His son, Jesus Christ, to be crucified for our sins.

Implementing the Strategy

7 Reflective Questions to Seize the Day on the Battlefield

1. What worthwhile opportunities have been presented to me that I have not seized? Attack them at once!

2. What people or things have I allowed to distract me from seizing very important opportunities? Determine to no longer allow those distractions to interfere with your progress.

3. What one opportunity could I act on tomorrow, which would have the greatest impact on my life? Make a decision to act on it.

4. What one thing has God called me to do that I have omitted, neglected, or procrastinated in getting done? Begin taking steps toward it immediately.

5. What successful opportunity have I acted on in the past that yielded great success for me? Build on that victory. Give yourself plenty of credit for your accomplishment.

6. What past failures have I allowed to paralyze me and stop me from acting? Push those past failures aside and begin to act boldly with confidence.

7. How might my life be improved through the people around me? Surround yourself with people who love you, believe in you, support you, and are possibility thinkers. Remove yourself from faithless, negative people and environments to the best of your ability.

It is of vital importance that we maximize every day God has given to us. Let us always remember that it is God who has given us each day. The great inventor, statesman, and philosopher Benjamin Franklin once wrote, "Do not squander time, for it is the stuff that life is made of."

Now, you have the weapon. How are you going to use it?

Victory is mine! In the next 7 days, I will act on the following in order to Seize the Day!:

_____

_____

_____

_____

Chapter 21

Dream

"I have a dream."

-Dr. Martin Luther King, Jr.

"... I will pour out my Spirit on all people.
Your sons and daughters will prophesy,
your old men will dream dreams,
your young men will see visions."

-Joel 2:28

Weapon #20: Dream

Why It Is Powerful

If we are to be truly productive in fulfilling God's mission for our lives, it is vital that we dream. The great pastor and motivational speaker, Myles Munroe said this: "The poorest person on earth is the not the person without money, but without a dream." Have you ever noticed how alive people are when they have a dream in their heart? Their eyes light up when they begin to speak of their dreams. They become animated. It is as if every fiber of their being is leaping.

Contrarily, when we meet someone who has allowed their dream to die, it is as if something inside of them has died also. The light that was once in their eyes is gone along with their passion. What is the source of the light in the dreamer's eyes? There is light in their eyes and passion in their being because their dreams were placed in them by God. Dreams hold such power.

Dreams free us to be all that God created us to be. Dreams are the birthplaces of miracles and the liberators of our destinies. It is dreaming that causes us to achieve the impossible, even when others think it is not practical. It has been said that "optimists are the saviors of the world." I have often asked myself, "What makes dreaming so special?" I concluded that it was this great truth: No matter how bad my conditions may be today, there's a brighter day coming. Despite my past defeats, hurts, or time on the clock, I can still come back.

Here are some key truths about the power of a dream.

A Dream

- A dream properly understood is a snapshot of great things to come.

- A dream keeps you motivated and inspired with the expectation of something great.

- A dream guards you heart, mind, and spirit from a dry, dead, and mundane life.

- A dream will empower you to do your best work on the job.

- A dream is often misunderstood by people who live defensively and have little or no vision.

- A dream is a sure anchor in the storms of life.

- A dream, fully engaged and visualized, will expand your consciousness to possibility thinking.

- A dream comes from a multitude of business (Dreams don't tend to wait for people with no initiative.).

- A dream, like all living things, must be fed to survive.

- A dream strengthens our wings to break out of cocoons of containment and soar to our destinies.

If you don't decide on your own dream, one will be chosen for you, and it will probably be a nightmare. (You will forever be an extra in someone else's feature film.).

One need not look far in our nation to know how fascinated people are by dreams. Some of the greatest songs of all time celebrate dreaming. Songs like "The Impossible Dream," "Tomorrow," and "I Believe I Can Fly" send our imaginations into orbit. In addition, many of today's top rated television shows, such as "American Idol" and "The Contender" are basically the stories of ordinary people trying to fulfill extraordinary dreams.

I believe that deep within the heart of humankind, we all love a great comeback story. We love to the see the underdog go from rags to riches and succeed. That inward desire to want to see others succeed was placed there by God. Why? It is because God loves the underdog. You see, we were all unlikely underdogs who were destined for eternal failure. Yet, God, in His limitless love for us sent Jesus to die for our sins. Not only did He die for our salvation, but for our success, as well.

Today we live in a world that is characterized by gloom, doom, and prognostications of defeat. What's worse is that we who possess the good news of the Gospel are often the worst culprits. Far too often we are the killers of other people's dreams and sprits. This is quite a tragedy, particularly when Jesus came to spread the Good News. If anyone has anything to be joyful about, it ought to be Bible-believing Christians

WMP Q&A:

Q: Why is this defeatism the case? Why is the world so pessimistic?

A: We have given up on our dreams and have simply stopped dreaming.

We have relegated the Bible to nothing more than a book of nice children's stories and maxims, rather than the living, breathing words of life. We have relegated our dream to be a waste of time simply, instead of allowing it to catapult us into greatness. I like what the great philanthropist, speaker, and entrepreneur, Peter J. Daniels had to say about dreaming. "Dreaming is not a waste of time. When you dream, you're on the periphery of God-likeness because you're creating something out of nothing." It is clear. One of the most productive things that a man or woman can do is dream.

Strategy for Victory

Action 1: Dream Like a Child

Sometimes, children are the greatest dream teachers. Freed and unencumbered by the cares of this world, they allow their imaginations to soar. Young people tend to believe that anything is possible. Have you ever noticed how inquisitive and imaginative they are? Perhaps that is why Jesus said that unless we become like a little child, we cannot see the Kingdom of God. The wonder and awe of a child is something precious that we should never, ever lose.

A classic example of childhood optimism is the Broadway musical "Annie." Years ago, I had the pleasure of seeing this wonderful production. Annie is the eternal optimist. Despite the hurtful language, hardship, and conditions administered by her foster mother, she remains upbeat, never losing hope. Every night, she dreams of her parents coming back to get her. She stares out of the window and dreams about the parents who gave her up. She wonders what they are like and rationalizes why they left her. She also dreams about the new family that will one day adopt her. Against the odds she continues to dream. In the wonderful song, "Maybe," she sings:

"Maybe they're young, maybe they're smart,

Bet they collect things like ashtrays and art,

Maybe they're good, why shouldn't they be,

Their one mistake was givin' up me,

So maybe now it's time, and maybe when I wake,

They'll be there calling me baby,

Maybe."

As adults, we sometimes suffer from what is known as "information overload." In this condition, we become so inundated with data and facts that we fail to think creatively. The problem with this condition is that we tend to play it safe and not take risks. We often find ourselves becoming more fact-conscious, self preserving, and calculating, rather than faith conscious. This disposition is not a fertile atmosphere for dreaming because it is based on fear.

How many times have you met someone who was intelligent, but cold, self-preserving, and overly calculating? When we operate in this manner, we fail to exercise one of God's greatest gifts to us, the gift of faith. The Bible states at least four times in scripture that the "just shall live by faith." It is by faith that we please God. In fact, **Hebrews 11:6 says, "And without faith it is impossible to please God, because anyone who comes to him must believe that he exists and that he rewards those who earnestly seek him."** This passage reveals a vital component of how God involves Himself in the affairs of humankind. It's not enough for us merely to believe that God exists. How many people believe in the existence of God? The Bible tells us that "even the demons believe, and tremble." The real challenge comes with our belief that He will reward our faith and perseverance.

Many Christians, because of past hurts, disappointments, or failures, lose heart and lose faith. We must take God at God's Word. We must trust in Him, knowing that He wants above all things to bless. When our feelings change, God's word continues to remain the same. If we are to do great things for God, we must be courageous. How many times in the Bible does God remind us to "be strong and very courageous?" God did this to emphasize the fact that it takes courage to do great things and exercise faith. When we courageously dare to dream, we will see God do great things in our lives. Children dream often without realizing they are being courageous. We should take a cue from them.

I would like to make one important point in regard to facts. I believe that facts are vitally important. We should be well informed people, and we should definitely be in the business of fact-finding and fact-gathering. We should be armed with information, especially when making key decisions. However, we should not be limited by facts, thereby making decisions based on facts alone. Faith should be an important component in our decision-making, as well. Great decisions call for great faith. Albert Einstein once said, "Imagination is more important than facts." Einstein possessed a brilliant analytical mind and still emphasized the importance of imagination to discovery. Einstein knew that utilizing his exceptional imagination would not be an enemy of his work. He knew that imagination would enhance his work.

Action 2: Dream to Create a Dream

Harriet Tubman is one of my heroines. **Without** a doubt, she is a great example of someone who dared **to dream** despite the facts.

Tubman, solemnly referred to as "A Woman Called Moses," was responsible for leading over 300 enslaved people of African descent, referred to as "slaves," to freedom via the "Underground Railroad." Born Araminta Ross in Dorchester County, Maryland into slavery in 1813, purely of African descent, she was called "Harriet," after her mother by the age of twelve. Her name changed to Tubman when she was married.

Subjected to the harshest of conditions and the most violent of whippings, Tubman had a dream. She wanted to escape to the North to freedom. She was a woman of remarkable bravery and leadership, even at a young age. Once, for refusing to tie up someone who was accused of escaping from the plantation, Tubman was hit in the head with a metal weight by a white overseer. This injury would affect her for the rest of her life as she developed the sleeping disease of narcolepsy. Because of the effects of this disease, Tubman might instantly fall asleep at any given moment. Even with this disease, however, she would not be deterred from her dream of freedom.

Tubman loved her father, Benjamin Ross, a man of impeccable honesty and integrity. The enslavement of African people in America was full of irony. Indeed, it was a peculiar institution. Tubman's parents were able to hunt and fish. Her father was a skilled outdoorsman. When Tubman shared her dream of escaping with him, her father advised against it for safety reasons. Yet, he knew his determined daughter would follow through on her mission. He realized that if she was going to go through with it, she needed to learn some things. However, he did not want to know the details of her plans – should he ever be questioned about them. He put his trust for her life and safety into the hands of God. Ross knew the land and would teach Tubman the vital skills for survival. He would teach her how to survive on the right nuts and berries for nutrition. He would teach her how to follow the "North Star" that would take her northbound toward freedom.

Tubman incurred several narcoleptic spells during her escape. While asleep, she would dream. As she dreamed, the Holy Spirit would speak to her and give her directions as to which way to go. Tubman eventually escaped to the North. Her dream of freedom had become a reality through divine providence. When she made it to the North, an entirely new world opened up for her. To taste freedom was great, but it wasn't enough. You see Tubman had a heart for people. What about her family? What about the people she cared about? What would happen if she only thought of herself? Her dream then began to take on a life of its own. She would later receive cooperation for her cause through the assistance of the Quakers. The Quakers, because of their strong Christian beliefs in the individual rights of all, were abolitionists who helped her with her great dream.

Then, amazingly, Tubman discovered one of the greatest truths about a dream. She learned how God strategically places people in your life to assist you with your dream. Of all of the people she thought would help her, Tubman never imagined that they would be white people. It was an even bigger dream than her escaping. It was amazing to her that the promises in the Bible actually existed in real life. She was now experiencing a dream within a dream.

Tubman would later form the Underground Railroad and ensure the safe escape for hundreds of captive people. She was never caught, and even served the Union Army in the Civil War. This great Woman of God will be forever remembered as a heroine and symbol of strength, freedom, courage, and vision. Against all odds, she dared to make her dream of freedom a reality. Because of her courage to follow her dream of freedom, she experienced so many other dreams within that dream. She will go down in history as one of the world's greatest dreamers. Will you too have the courage to make your dream a reality? All creation awaits!

Action 3: Assemble Your Dream Team

One of the most vital and underutilized benefits of productivity is the assembly of a Dream Team. What is a Dream Team? A dream team consists of those individuals whom God has assembled to assist you in the realization of your dream or goal. This concept and name became famous during the 1992 Olympic Games in Barcelona, Spain. After the United States basketball team finished a dismal third place at the 1988 Summer Olympics in Seoul, Korea, America had lost its dream of basketball dominance. In 1992, professionals from the National Basketball Association (NBA) were allowed to compete in the Olympics for the first time in the Games' history.

Team USA, coached by legendary Detroit Pistons coach Chuck Day, consisted of some of the NBA's all-time greats such as Michael Jordan, Larry Bird, Magic Johnson, and David Robinson. Some considered this team to be the greatest basketball team ever assembled. During the series of competitions, they won their games by an average of nearly fifty points a game. As a result of assembling this great team, the US easily won the Gold Medal, defeating Croatia.

The dream was realized. Players played their positions flawlessly as they gelled together, hand-in-glove, participating with precision. The important point is how easily the Dream Team won the Gold Medal.

When I first heard about the Dream Team being formed, I had no doubt that they would win. I mean, what would anyone expect from the greatest professional team of all time? To that end, when the Dream Team won the Gold medal, I was not impressed. I hate to admit it, but it is true. Then again, who was I to challenge the ruling that allowed professional athletes to compete and win? If the Fédération Internationale de Basketball (International Basketball Federation/ FIBA), the sanctioning body, determined the NBA players' eligibility, who was I to dispute their decision? No rules were broken at all. We had a dream of winning the Gold Medal, we assembled a team, and we won. Case closed!

This kind of thinking is typical amongst many Christians. We sometimes don't accept opportunities or circumstances because they seem too easy or too good to be true. That martyr mentality – determined to earn everything with great suffering – is a clever trick of the devil. God may have designed a plan for you to achieve sweat-less victory! Take it!

Just as that team was assembled to realize the dream of winning the gold, God has assigned a Dream Team specifically for you. They have been placed in your life to enable you not only to realize your dream, but to realize it easier, faster, smarter, and better than you could have on your own.

Consider the following questions:

• Are you working harder than you have to?

• Are you an amateur in trying to do something that someone you know is gifted in?

• Has pride prohibited you from asking for help from people who love you and would be delighted to assist you?

If you answered, "Yes," to any of these questions, it is time to be prayerful about your Dream Team. Ask God to show you the people God has prepared to help you live God's will for your life. Remember, some of them could be the people you least expect, but trust that God knows what talents God has given to each of us.

This concept of the Dream Team is **not a new concept.** The great Napoleon Hill, author of the timeless classic *Think and Grow Rich* called it the "Master Mind." Hill defined the Master Mind as "the coordination of knowledge and effort, in a spirit of harmony, between two or more people, for the attainment of a definite purpose." It was this concept that was responsible for building some of the largest empires in the United States. Through this concept, Henry Ford overcame poverty, illiteracy, and ignorance to become one of the wealthiest men in the world, and the pioneer of auto mass production.

Another famous person who used this concept was perhaps the greatest inventor of all time, Thomas Edison. Despite only finishing grade school Edison invented not only the light bulb, but countless other inventions while amassing a fortune through this concept. Ford and Edison were not only contemporaries, but they were such close friends that Edison had a laboratory at the Ford headquarters in Dearborn, Michigan. These titans of industry certainly possessed talent, but were it not for the assembly of their Dream Teams, we may well have never read about them. Will we one day read about you?

As you seek to assemble this great league of men and women, you will be amazed at what God does with your obedience.

Are you ready to assemble your Dream Team? Here is how:

- Select people who truly care about you, and want to see you succeed.

- Choose individuals who already possess their own visions and dreams, and are experiencing success in their own lives.

- Ensure that the people you choose have a gift that can truly add to your dream.

- Guarantee that they have no ulterior motive in helping you, and they are without envy and jealousy.

- Don't select "Yes" people. Make sure you have people who are bold enough to be honest with you. Make sure that you are ready to receive constructive feedback. Remember, they are not on your team to agree with you on everything, but to make you better.

- Welcome their differences in personality. They don't need to be like you; on the contrary, their unique differences bring objectivity and value.

Be sure to reciprocate. Be committed to assist them by contributing your gifts and talents to them as well.

As I write the final chapters of this book, it gives me great pleasure to write about my Dream Team. I must tell you that I had no concept of how to get this book edited, published, or even sold. However, as I was obedient to God to simply write it and pray for people to help me, the key people began to show up. The first was Marjé Etheridge, my Marketing Director and Publicist. As **Habakkuk 2:2** says, **"Write the vision and make it plain, that others may see it and run with it."**

I met Marjé while I was speaking at a youth event she organized. I didn't see her for a while, but when I ran into her again I shared the concept for my book with her. Marjé had formerly been the Marketing Director for one of the largest churches in metropolitan Atlanta. Immediately, upon the mention of the book, she caught the vision and ran with it. She was so excited about the book that she told everyone. I didn't have all of the money that I really wanted to pay her at the time, but she didn't care. She was sold on the concept of the book. Almost daily we would talk about the book and the ideas that she had for speaking engagements, and other events. She even began to assemble a team of capable people for me and around me. Marjé and her husband, Carl are fellow church members, and priceless confidants. Marjé has become the big sister that I never had. Regrettably, she lost her younger brother to gang violence. I have been honored, in turn to become the little brother in place of the one she tragically lost.

Through this process, I have learned that with God, you don't have to have all of the answers. It is vital, however, that you have a willing heart and move by faith in the right direction.

Implementing the Strategy

7 Tactics to Dream on the Battlefield

1. Identify the environment most conducive to you being inspired to dream? Determine to immerse yourself in that environment, and you will be amazed at what happens.

2. Name the dreamers you admire most in history. I believe God has assigned heroes of history that we connect with in a special way. Study their lives and what inspired them to dream.

3. Do something! Dreaming begins to take on form and flesh with every act in the direction of your dream. Take tangible steps in the direction of your dreams! Listen to this great quote by Henry David Thoreau: "If one advances confidently in the direction of his [or her] dreams, and endeavors to live the life which he [or she] has imagined, he [or she] will meet with a fate unexpected in common hours." Run with confidence toward your dream!

4. If you don't know what dream God has placed in your life, ask Him to reveal it to you. James 1:5 says, "If any of you lacks wisdom, you should ask God, who gives generously to all without finding fault, and it will be given to you."

5. Ask yourself this question: What is it that frustrates you the most? Perhaps you are the one who God is raising up to solve this problem. How much peace of mind would you have knowing that this problem was solved? Mohandas Gandhi said, "We must become the solution we seek in the world." Don't see yourself as being too small to act.

6. Surround yourself with other dreamers. Great minds tend to think alike. Talk to others about their dreams and encourage them. You will be amazed at the synergy that takes place. Your "Dream Team" has been assigned by God to help you.

7. Remove yourself from negative environments and people that stifle, ridicule, and shoot down your dreams. A dream is a precious gift from God. Handle it with care. Some of these people, surprisingly, may be family members. Focus on giving birth to your dream and eliminating distractions. Satan is after your dream and will use anyone to destroy it. Joseph was ridiculed by his brothers for his dream. Nevertheless, remember it was his dream that saved not only his family and Egypt, but humankind.

Dreams are gifts from God. We should open them with great expectation and partner with God to make them come true.

Now, you have the weapon. How are you going to use it?

Victory is mine! In the next 7 days, I will act on the following to make my Dream a reality:

_____

_____

_____

_____

Chapter 22

You Gotta Have Heart

*"Courage is the finest of human qualities
because it is the quality that guarantees all others."*
-Winston Churchill

"Be strong and courageous."
-Deuteronomy 31:6

Weapon #21: You Gotta Have Heart

Why It Is Powerful

Finally, we have come to the twenty-first weapon. It is one that must be in your arsenal for the other twenty weapons to be effective. It is this: You gotta have heart!: "You gotta have heart!" You must be courageous. The word "courage," comes from the French root word "coeur," which means "heart." As the heart is the life-source of the body, courage is the life-source of the other virtues according to author Tim Hansel. As the heart pumps life to the body through the blood, courage pumps life to all of the other virtues.

Courage is of vital importance for a number of reasons. First, it takes courage to exercise your faith. The Bible says in **Hebrews 11:6, "And without faith it is impossible to please God..."** "Courage" or "courageous" is mentioned thirty-five times in the Bible. The term "Be strong," or a reference to it, is mentioned approximately 230 times. Since faith is required to please God, it is vital you have courage.

Second, it takes courage to love. Love is the highest of all qualities in the Kingdom of God. Love is God's economy. In fact, the Word tells us that "Faith worketh by love." Love for humankind was God's motive for sending His son Jesus to die for our sins. Calvary was the ultimate battle, and Jesus was the world's greatest warrior. He forever set the example for leadership and battle strategy, and love was his weapon.

We must have courage if we are going to fulfill the mission God has for our lives. The question has been often asked, "What makes the great great?" When asked this very question, Peter J. Daniels responded, "It's a sense of destiny." In other words, the belief that you were placed here on planet earth to do something of significance for God and humankind is what separates mediocrity from magnificence. Courage may well be the chief component of greatness. It takes courage to live out one's destiny. It also takes courage to persevere. It takes courage to love, and it takes courage to live this great life that God intended for you to live.

In our society there is an epidemic that gnaws at the very fiber of our existence. This great cancer kills dreams and destroys lives that were originally destined for greatness. This disease causes men and women to play it safe in life, living lives of containment. What is this disease? Self preservation! William Shakespeare said, "Cowards die many times before their deaths; the valiant never taste death but once."

As I consider the lives of the great, I see this crimson thread that runs through their lives. It is in some ways similar to my hero and savior, Jesus, and it is this: a willingness to die for what one believes in. The great Martin Luther King, Jr. said, "Unless a man has discovered something he is willing to die for, he is not fit to live." Helen Keller, the great educator who was both deaf and blind, said, "Avoiding danger is no safer in the long run than outright exposure.

The fearful are caught as often as the bold. Life is a daring adventure or nothing at all." As I conclude this final chapter, I would like to leave you with this final weapon and admonition: **Live your life to the fullest and don't cheapen your existence by self-preservation.** Your life was not meant to be lived in black and white, but in vivid, spectacular Technicolor! You must fight **Satan** for your destiny, and he will not relinquish it easily. Consider this quote from Joan of Arc. This great woman of God, who believed she heard a voice from God, terrorized the English Angevine Empire at only seventeen years of age. Because of her beliefs to reclaim her homeland of France from English rule, she scored major victories in battle. She was finally captured and offered the opportunity to live and renounce her actions. Instead she chose to die for her beliefs.

Listen to these final words of courage: "One life is all we have and we live it as we believe in living it. But to sacrifice what you are, and to live without belief, that is a fate more terrible than dying." Because of her beliefs, she was willing to die. By being willing to die, she inspired many others to be willing to die, as well.

Yet, there is one much greater than Joan of Arc who gave his life so that we might live life abundantly. He hung on a cross and was crucified for the entire sins of humankind. He not only died for you, but He gave you power, authority, and dominion over this earth, and our enemy, Satan. Your victory is on the horizon as his disciple. His one requirement to be his disciple is that you "Take up your cross daily, deny yourself and follow me." His greatest desire is not just that you have the courage to die for Him. His greatest desire is that you have the courage to fulfill His plan for your life and live for him!

Implementing the Strategy

7 Tactics to Have Heart on the Battlefield

1. **Study the Word of God** – Read God's word daily. It is the world's most timeless, alive, and enduring document ever written. In it lies the solution to all of life's problems. It s not a novel. To quote Kenneth Copeland, "It is a 66-volume victory statement!"

2. **Consider Others** – What cause has God given you a heart and passion for whereby you can bless others? Get outside of yourself. The essence of who you are is yet to be revealed when courage comes forth on behalf of others.

3. **Risk** – Don't play it safe all of the time. Jesus' great commandment is the commandment of love. You can't live in a bunker. For there to be sacrifice to God, it should cost you something.

4. **Accountability** – Who do you have in your life that stretches your courage for Christ and challenges you to live for Him? Ensure that you have some high-flying eagles around you. Build strength in your wings and soar.

5. **Boldly Stand Up For Right!** – There is nothing more strengthening to one's courage than taking a stand on an unpopular issue for Christ. You may think your boss is looking for a cowardly yes-man or woman, but that's probably not accurate. They are looking for ethical leaders that people will follow.

6. **Study the Courageous** – Biographies have been an incredible source for changing people's lives in a profound way. Read yourself into history. Listen to audio books and watch videos of the great. Let it get in your spirit. If you have a favorite person in history, you can use them as model for how you'd like to be.

7. **Pray for Boldness** – in your prayer time, pray and ask God to give you boldness. This was the prayer that the disciples prayed for service. Pray that He will reveal to you your assignment

Live a fearless life! God wants to see you, God's child, thrive.

Now, you have the weapon. How are you going to use it?

Victory is mine! In the next 7 days, I will act on the following in order to Have Heart:

_____

_____

_____

_____

Conclusion

Congratulations on your accomplishment in completing this book. My hope is that your life and productivity have been enriched. I sincerely hope that, as result of reading this book, you stand taller, live bigger, and become greater than you ever imagined. It's been an honor and a privilege being your war buddy. I have enjoyed our 21-day journey, as together we have walked toward your destiny.

Each weapon has some unique piece of the puzzle for your arsenal. I recommend that you not merely read this book once, and lay it on the shelf, but read it again and again. Let it refresh and inspire you when needed. Use it as a reference tool, manual, and as a devotional. I hope that you will read it to your children to teach them that, as a man or woman of Christ, we are engaged in constant warfare. Pass it on as a gift to friends and loved ones, who you desire to see with improved and enriched lives.

It is my hope also, that of the 21 weapons, you select your favorites. Read them to inspire and encourage yourself whenever you need a lift. Be objective about those areas where you may need improvement. Remember that the areas where we need the most improvement are not always the ones we enjoy. As we approach our jobs and businesses tomorrow, let's face the day with a renewed spirit, attitude, mind, and heart. As you go, march boldly into the marketplace, understanding that whatever your profession, you have a high and holy calling. Royal blood flows through your veins and your destiny is greatness! All creation waits, as your greatness is manifested as a son and daughter of God. God bless you and remember that your BEST is yet to come!

An Invitation

It is at this point in our journey that I offer you the greatest of invitations. For more than 21 days, we have discussed battle strategy, God, and how to operate as a great soldier. We have discussed the importance of God, destiny, work, family, success, and war. Having said that, it would be impossible to talk about war without introducing you to the greatest warrior who ever lived. I am speaking of none other than Jesus Christ. He was the ultimate warrior, and love was his ultimate weapon. He died for your sins so that you could experience the abundant life. He came to give His life so that you could live eternally. I could not have written this book without the great liberty that only He can give. I now invite you to accept Him as your Lord and Savior and to live the fearless life. If you would like to accept him please pray this prayer:

Lord Jesus, thank you for dying for my sins on the cross and loving me. Your precious blood cleanses me of every sin. I believe that you rose from the dead and that you are alive today. I accept you as my Savior today. Because of your finished work I am a child of God and I thank you for eternal life and for filling my heart with peace, joy, and love. Amen.

Bibliography

Abdulla, Sara. "Miserable Monday." Nature News 21 Jan. 2000. 13 May 2010. <http://www.nature.com/news/2000/000121/full/news000127-1.html>

Bennett, William J., ed. The Book of Virtues: A Treasury of Great Moral Stories. New York: Simon and Schuster, 1993.

Caruso, Kevin. "Suicide Most Likely on Mondays, According to UK Study." Online posting. 25 Aug. 2005. 13 May 2010. <http://www.suicide.org/suicide-most-likely-on-mondays.html>

Covey, Stephen R. The Seven Habits of Highly Effective People: Restoring the Character Ethic. New York: Simon and Schuster, 1989.

Daniels, Peter J. How to Reach Your Life Goals. Adelaide, South Australia: The House of Tabor. 1985.

Goleman, Daniel. Emotional Intelligence. New York: Bantam, 1995.

Hansel, Tim. You Gotta Keep Dancin': In the midst of life's hurts, you can choose joy. Audio recording. Lifejourney Books, 1987.

Hill, Napoleon. Think and Grow Rich. Audio recording. Penguin Audio, 2008.

Lucas, Jr., Jimmie L. Custom-Built By God: Originals Are Worth More Than Copies. Riverdale: QIM Publishing, 2005.

Maxwell, John C. Put Your Dream to the Test: 10 Questions That Will Help You See It and Seize It. Nashville: Thomas Nelson, 2009.

Mohammed. "The Universal Law of Attraction." Online posting. 11 Jan. 2007. 13 May 2010.
<http://www.livethepower.com/blog/2007/01/the-universal-law-of-attraction>

"Monday Morning Bad for Your Health." CNN Online. 3 Feb. 2005. 13 May 2010.
<http://edition.cnn.com/2005/BUSINESS/02/03/monday.pressure/index.html>

Munroe, Myles. Kingdom Principles: Preparing for Kingdom Experience and Expansion. Shippensburg: Destiny Image Publishers, 2006.

Murdock, Mike. The Making of a Champion: 31 Power Keys to Unleashing Your Personal Greatness. Fort Worth: The Wisdom Center, 2002.

---. Unstoppable Passion. Fort Worth: The Wisdom Center, 2007.

---. Wisdom For Crisis Times: Master Keys for Success in Times of Change. Denton: The Wisdom Center, 1992.

Nee, Watchman. The Spiritual Man. Anaheim: Living Stream Ministry, 1992.

Nightingale, Earl. The Strangest Secret. Audio recording. Earl Nightingale, 2011.

"Only 45% of Workers Are Satisfied With Their Jobs, A Record Low: Survey." Huffington Post 5 Jan. 2010. 13 May 2010.
<http://www.huffingtonpost.com/2010/01/05/american-job-satisfaction_n_411680.html>

Thompson, Robb. Excellence in Attitude. Tinley Park: Family Harvest Church, 2002.